DAVID WILLIAMSON's first full-length play, *The Coming of Stork*, premiered at the La Mama Theatre, Carlton, in 1970 and later became the film *Stork*, directed by Tim Burstall.

The Removalists and *Don's Party* followed in 1971, then *Jugglers Three* (1972), *What If You Died Tomorrow?* (1973), *The Department* (1975), *A Handful of Friends* (1976), *The Club* (1977) and *Travelling North* (1979). In 1972 *The Removalists* won the Australian Writers' Guild AWGIE Award for best stage play and the best script in any medium and the British production saw Williamson nominated most promising playwright by the London *Evening Standard*.

The 1980s saw his success continue with *Celluloid Heroes* (1980), *The Perfectionist* (1982), *Sons of Cain* (1985), *Emerald City* (1987) and *Top Silk* (1989); whilst the 1990s produced *Siren* (1990), *Money and Friends* (1991), *Brilliant Lies* (1993), *Sanctuary* (1994), *Dead White Males* (1995), *Heretic* (1996), *Third World Blues* (an adaptation of *Jugglers Three*) and *After the Ball* (both in 1997), and *Corporate Vibes* and *Face to Face* (both in 1999). *The Great Man* (2000), *Up for Grabs*, *A Conversation*, *Charitable Intent* (all in 2001), *Soulmates* (2002), *Birthrights* (2003), *Amigos, Flatfoot* (both in 2004), *Scarlett O'Hara at the Crimson Parrot* (2008) and *Let the Sunshine* (2009) have since followed.

Williamson is widely recognised as Australia's most successful playwright and over the last thirty years his plays have been performed throughout Australia and produced in Britain, United States, Canada and many European countries. A number of his stage works have been adapted for the screen, including *The Removalists, Don's Party, The Club, Travelling North, Emerald City, Sanctuary* and *Brilliant Lies*.

David Williamson has won the Australian Film Institute film script award for *Petersen* (1974), *Don's Party* (1976), *Gallipoli* (1981) and *Travelling North* (1987) and has won eleven Australian Writers' Guild AWGIE Awards. He lives on Queensland's Sunshine Coast with his writer wife, Kristin Williamson.

SCARLETT O'HARA AT THE CRIMSON PARROT & LET THE SUNSHINE

DAVID WILLIAMSON

Currency Press, Sydney

CURRENCY PLAYS

First published in 2009
by Currency Press Pty Ltd,
PO Box 2287, Strawberry Hills, NSW, 2012, Australia
enquiries@currency.com.au
www.currency.com.au

Copyright: *Scarlett O'Hara at the Crimson Parrot* © David Williamson, 2008; *Let the Sunshine* © David Williamson, 2009.

COPYING FOR EDUCATIONAL PURPOSES

The Australian *Copyright Act 1968* (Act) allows a maximum of one chapter or 10% of this book, whichever is the greater, to be copied by any educational institution for its educational purposes provided that that educational institution (or the body that administers it) has given a remuneration notice to Copyright Agency Limited (CAL) under the Act.

For details of the CAL licence for educational institutions contact CAL, Level 15, 233 Castlereagh Street, Sydney NSW 2000; Ph 1800 066 844; email info@copyright.com.au

COPYING FOR OTHER PURPOSES

Except as permitted under the Act, for example a fair dealing for the purposes of study, research, criticism or review, no part of this book may be reproduced, stored in a retrieval system, or transmitted in any form or by any means without prior written permission. All enquiries should be made to the publisher at the address above.

Any performance or public reading of *Scarlett O'Hara at the Crimson Parrot* or *Let the Sunshine* is forbidden unless a licence has been received from the author or the author's agent. The purchase of this book in no way gives the purchaser the right to perform the plays in public, whether by means of a staged production or reading. All applications for public performance should be addressed to the author, c/- Cameron Cresswell Agency, info@cameronsmanagement.com.au, ph 9389 3819, fax 9387 4078.

NATIONAL LIBRARY OF AUSTRALIA CIP DATA

Author:	Williamson, David, 1942–.
Title:	Two plays: Scarlett O'Hara at the Crimson Parrot and Let the Sunshine / David Williamson.
ISBN:	978 0 86819 865 1 (pbk.)
Dewey Number:	A822.3

Typeset by Dean Nottle for Currency Press.
Cover design by Emma Vine, Currency Press.
Front cover shows Georgie Parker, William Zappa, Kate Raison, Andrew McFarlane in the 2009 Ensemble Theatre production of *Let the Sunshine* (photo by Steve Lunam), and Caroline O'Connor and Andrew McFarlane in the 2008 MTC production of *Scarlett O'Hara at the Crimson Parrot* (photo by Jeff Busby)

Contents

SCARLETT O'HARA AT THE CRIMSON PARROT

Foreword
   Simon Phillips   *3*

  Act One   7
  Act Two   47

LET THE SUNSHINE

Foreword
   Sandra Bates   *83*

  Act One   87
  Act Two   121

Currency Press acknowledges the Traditional Owners of the Country on which we live and work. We pay our respects to all Aboriginal and Torres Strait Islander Elders, past and present.

Publication of this title was assisted by the Commonwealth Government through the Australia Council, its arts funding and advisory body.

SCARLETT O'HARA
AT THE CRIMSON PARROT

Foreword

Simon Phillips

Two icons of the Australian theatre are hard to resist, even when they approach you batting eyelids with little more than a glint behind them. So when perennially popular social satirist David Williamson and prima comedienne and music theatre star Caroline O'Connor told me they wanted to tailor a work together to showcase O'Connor's abundant skills, I jumped on board for the mystery ride.

I'd already commissioned a work for O'Connor by Joanna Murray-Smith, designed to emphasise her delightful versatility as an actress rather than her all-singing-all-dancing virtuosity, so I had no doubts about her ability to rise to this new challenge. David, on the other hand, inspired by the talent and charms of his muse, was attempting something quite out of his comfort zone, a comedy of style rather than bad manners, structured towards romance rather than his customary testosterone-fuelled abuse.

But the form of the idea was so interesting—with its Walter Mittyesque fantasies depending on an artful use of film—that we all embarked on its development with zest.

I won't say it was an easy ride, but it was the more invigorating *because* we were attempting something new, and David's unerring sense of the audience's funny-bone (he didn't *entirely* abandon his tried-and-true chauvinists and matriarchs) coupled with Caroline's truly brilliant sense of comic invention resulted in an evening which saw capacity houses consistently cackling and frequently convulsed with laughter.

The nature of that event in the theatre may not be fully communicated in a printed text, for if theatre is always a team effort and a combination of creative forces, this was never truer than in the case of *Scarlett*. As with many new works the contribution made by the original cast is inestimable (joining Caroline were Matt Day, Bob Hornery, Andrew

McFarlane, Marney McQueen, Monica Maughan and Simon Wood) and I feel compelled in particular to acknowledge the superb effort put in by my staff at the Melbourne Theatre Company, who created the sets, costumes and wigs necessary to morph the actors into so many Hollywood classics. I'm only sorry that this text can't in some way contain the truly gorgeous and hilarious series of clips created by Josh Burns, Matt Scott, Benjamin Hidalgo and Elvis Pramod Vittal in just three days of intensive filming.

Be that as it may, I'm sure it remains a robust tribute to the triumph of the heart over the hum-drum, the dreamers over the nay-sayers and, theatrically, of two determined icons over the expected.

Simon Phillips, Melbourne, July 2009

Simon Phillips
November 2009

Scarlett O'Hara at the Crimson Parrot was first produced by Melbourne Theatre Company at the Victorian Arts Centre Playhouse, Melbourne, on 7 June 2008 with the following cast:

ALAN	Matt Day
GORDON	Bob Hornery
MAUREEN	Monica Maughan
STEVE	Andrew McFarlane
SHELLEY	Marney McQueen
SCARLETT O'HARA	Caroline O'Connor
SIMON WOOD	Simon Wood

Director, Simon Phillips
LX Designer, Matt Scott
Composer, Ian McDonald
Designer, Shaun Gurton

CHARACTERS

SCARLETT O'HARA
MAUREEN
STEVE
GARY
GORDON
SHELLEY
ALAN

ACT ONE

SCENE ONE: GETTING ESTABLISHED

Scarlett's place. A small flat she shares with her mother. It's a tidy flat, almost too tidy and ordered. Rows of DVDs along the wall. She's facing us as she watches a film. It's late at night. We can't see what she's watching on her screen as it faces away from us, but we can see what she's seeing projected on a large screen at the rear of the stage. She's watching Casablanca *as Humphrey Bogart, as Rick, and Ingrid Bergman, as Ilsa, act out a classic scene. She mouths the words she already knows by heart.*

INGRID: I love you so much, and I hate this war so much. Oh, it's a crazy world. Anything can happen. If you shouldn't get away, I mean, if, if something should keep us apart, wherever they put you and wherever I'll be, I want you to know…

She can't go on. She lifts her face to his. He kisses her gently.

Kiss me. Kiss me as if it were the last time.

He looks into her eyes, then he does kiss her as though it were going to be the last time.

The tears are pouring out of SCARLETT*'s eyes. She grabs for tissues to try and stem the flood. Behind her, her mother* MAUREEN *appears.*

MAUREEN: *Casablanca*, again?

On screen, Ilsa's hand falls to the table and knocks over a glass.

SCARLETT *flicks off the DVD and stares at the screen, refusing to turn and face her mother.*

It's two thirty in the morning!

SCARLETT: Mum, it's my life.

MAUREEN: It's your life, but I do the worrying.

SCARLETT: Mum, I'm fine.

MAUREEN: It's not a natural life. You start work at five in the afternoon and get home at midnight. It's not a natural life.

SCARLETT: It's better than nine to five in retail.
MAUREEN: What was so wrong with retail?
SCARLETT: The compulsory smile. [*She does the fixed sales smile and imitates herself talking to a customer with it on.*] 'No, I'm terribly sorry, madam, we haven't got this in size twenty-two. What do we have? There's a nice yellow and blue striped tent in outdoor lifestyle, Floor Six.'
MAUREEN: When you suffer, I suffer. In my heart you're still that little girl who came running to me with bleeding knees.
SCARLETT: Mum, I'm thirty-six and—
MAUREEN: Bleeding knees. Always the bleeding knees. Band-aids? I spent a fortune.
SCARLETT: You were a very caring mother, but…
MAUREEN: I've never known a child so accident prone. That hasn't changed.
SCARLETT: I'm thirty-six—
MAUREEN: I just want to see you happy and settled before God taps my shoulder.
SCARLETT: Mum, you'll be around for years.
MAUREEN: No I won't. Not after what Dr Carstairs said today.
SCARLETT: [*stopping guiltily*] Was it today?
MAUREEN: Yes, today.
SCARLETT: I thought it was next…
MAUREEN: No, he brought the appointment forward. He was so worried he brought the appointment forward. I told you.
SCARLETT: Did you? I'm sorry. What did he say?
MAUREEN: Not good news.
SCARLETT: What?
MAUREEN: Not good news.
SCARLETT: Tell me.
MAUREEN: No, not tonight. It's too painful. We'll talk about it tomorrow.
SCARLETT: What? What did he say?
MAUREEN: My bones are so brittle I could snap like a reed in the wind. [*She snaps her fingers.*] Like a reed.
SCARLETT: You look fine.
MAUREEN: Darling, I'm nearly one and a half standard deviations below peak bone mass. And if my heart doesn't improve I'm going to have to get a pacemaker.

ACT ONE

SCARLETT: Are you sure he knows what he's talking about?
MAUREEN: He trained here. He's not an Indian.
SCARLETT: You seem fine.
MAUREEN: Call him if you don't believe what I'm telling you.

> *Tears stream from her eyes.* SCARLETT *approaches her mother to comfort her, then at the last moment feels embarrassed and backs off. It's a situation she often has to handle but she's still not quite got the hang of it.*

Would it hurt if you put your arms around your mother once in a while? When she's distressed?
SCARLETT: No, no. No.

> *She hurries to put her arms around her mother.*

MAUREEN: Not that hard. My bones, dear. My bones.

> SCARLETT *disengages hastily.*

SCARLETT: Sorry. Sorry.
MAUREEN: They wanted me to have you terminated...
SCARLETT: Yes, I know.
MAUREEN: I said no. This little life is too precious. Then they said you have to have her adopted to someone who really wants her, and I said, 'I really want her'.
SCARLETT: Yes, I know.
MAUREEN: The pressure was intense, I can't begin to tell you, but as soon as I set eyes on you I knew I was right. You were such a beautiful little thing. You're still attractive now of course, but when you were young... oh my God, people would stop, turn in the streets. Stare.
SCARLETT: I'm sorry I didn't turn out to be Vivien Leigh.
MAUREEN: I just wanted you to be something more than... a waitress.
SCARLETT: It's called earning a living, Mum.
MAUREEN: But the hours? How can you ever find a man? Mavis Arnott has five grandchildren, and she prattles on about them all the time. She's sticking a knife into an open wound and she knows it.
SCARLETT: Mum, I...
MAUREEN: You'd make a wonderful mother. Girls who've been well mothered themselves always do.
SCARLETT: Yeah.

MAUREEN: My only regret is you didn't have a father, but for some reason or other I never had the knack of making men want to stick around.

SCARLETT: A real mystery.

MAUREEN: I just want things to be better for you.

SCARLETT: I'm really quite happy.

MAUREEN: I'm a mother. I can see the sadness behind the brave face.

SCARLETT: [*defiantly*] I'm happy!

MAUREEN: You always had dreams. When you were five you yearned to be a ballerina.

SCARLETT: After my first lesson the teacher said, 'Dear, hard work can overcome everything except a total lack of co-ordination'.

MAUREEN: And you really wanted to sing.

SCARLETT: And I couldn't hold a tune. In fact I couldn't even find the tune I was meant to be holding. I'm sure there's something I'm potentially brilliant at, but I still haven't found it, and in the meantime I'm doing what I can.

MAUREEN: [*with a sigh*] I know, dear, I know. I'm not being judgemental. I'll see you in the morning.

She goes towards her room.

SCARLETT: [*almost in tears*] I'm doing what I can.

MAUREEN *turns at her doorway.*

MAUREEN: I know, dear. [*A sudden thought*] Oh. Tomorrow.

SCARLETT: [*wearily, she knows what's coming*] Yes.

MAUREEN: If it's not too much trouble. Dr Carstairs recommended this new inflatable headrest. I'm sorry, it's quite expensive, but he swears I'll sleep a whole lot better.

SCARLETT: I'll get it.

MAUREEN: You'll have to catch a train out to the warehouse in Reservoir.

SCARLETT: Reservoir?

MAUREEN: I'd go myself except if I slipped and fell getting on the train, it would probably be the end.

SCARLETT: Okay, okay, I'll go.

MAUREEN: And just one more thing—

SCARLETT: Mum, I can't afford to be late for work again.

MAUREEN: Alright, then. I can do without.

SCARLETT: What do you want?

MAUREEN: I was hoping for some new books from the library. But don't worry, I can read the ones I've got again.
SCARLETT: I'll get some more.
MAUREEN: You know the sort I like.
SCARLETT: Big print, bodice-rippers.
MAUREEN: Adult romance. [*She's about to go, then thinks of something else.*] There was one other thing, but it's not important.
SCARLETT: What?
MAUREEN: More underwear. You know the type.
SCARLETT: Bloomers.
MAUREEN: Loose fit. But if you're too rushed…
SCARLETT: I'll get them.
MAUREEN: Darling, I know at times I seem like I'm nagging, but it comes from the heart. All I want in life is for you to be happy. We can't all be rich and famous but we can all try to rise above our limitations.

> MAUREEN *goes into her bedroom.* SCARLETT *stares straight ahead. Her mind wanders to the scene from* Rebecca *where Mrs Danvers tries to convince Rebecca to jump from the window.*

SCENE TWO: RESTAURANT RULES

The following day, 6.45 p.m.

We're in the kitchen of a restaurant and it's frantic. The kitchen is basic and small. There's no bar and the meagre wine list is stacked in a wine rack and the coolroom doubles as a beer and white wine cooler. The chef, STEVE, *is also the owner. He's frantically running from the grill to the stove to the oven as he struggles to keep up with the orders. He's assisted by the sous chef,* GARY, *a man in his early thirties, in his own eyes God's gift to women. Also working there is* GORDON, *an older man who washes dishes. His sink is downstage left.* SHELLEY, *twenty-eight and blonde, who fancies herself as God's gift to men, comes through the one part of the restaurant we can see. A single unoccupied banquette can be seen near the door of the kitchen. The rest of the dining area is offstage right and we can hear the buzz of diners coming from it.* SHELLEY *enters the door into the kitchen with dirty plates and places them on the tray.* STEVE *looks up expectantly.*

SHELLEY: Two rump steak, medium-to-well.
STEVE: Did you go through the specials?
SHELLEY: Yes.
STEVE: Did you?...
SHELLEY: Yes!
STEVE: You can't have been very convincing. Pitch it to me!
SHELLEY: Steve, they don't want them!
STEVE: Pitch it to me.
SHELLEY: We have two very special specials tonight. The chargrilled kangaroo sirloin with quandong chilli glaze and the emu fillet with riberry jus. And for dessert a delicious wattle seed pavlova.
STEVE: Put some passion into it, Shelley! I've got a coolroom stuffed with kangaroo and emu and it's not moving.
SHELLEY: Steve, I could offer them my body and they still wouldn't order that shit.
GARY: Might swing the balance now and then.

    SHELLEY *gives him the finger.*

STEVE: [*to* SHELLEY] You're ashamed of the produce of your own country?
SHELLEY: Let's add dingo and wombat.
GARY: I warned you, Steve.
STEVE: Gary, shut the fuck up!
GARY: You tried 'em. They didn't work. Get 'em off the menu.
STEVE: Gary, if you don't push the boundaries you die. Creatively you die.
GARY: You pushed the boundaries and we're dying.
STEVE: [*enraged*] Okay, if those cretins out there have no interest in expanding their culinary range, then let's just throw a few lumps of bovine bum on the grill... [*he does, it sizzles*] and cook the crap out of them until they're so tough they'll need a fucking chainsaw to eat 'em!
SHELLEY: [*as she picks up three meals* GARY *has plated earlier*] Table Nine's still waiting for their pork tenderloin and chicken in macadamia puree.
STEVE: It's coming! Where's Scarlett?!

    We see SCARLETT *racing past the empty banquette towards the kitchen. She's carrying her mother's errands in two big bags.*

Inevitably she goes to open the door just as SHELLEY *emerges with the three plates balanced on her arm.*

SHELLEY: Woah! [*To* SCARLETT] Sugar!
SCARLETT: Sorry, Shelley.
SHELLEY: Watch where you're going!
SCARLETT: So sorry I'm late, Steve.

She lets the door go, knocking the plates out of SHELLEY*'s hands. They crash to the floor out in the restaurant.*

GARY: Scarlett O'Hurricane!
SCARLETT: Are you alright, Shelley?
SHELLEY: Just go away.
STEVE: Scarlett, how many times do I have to tell you? In right, out right…
SCARLETT: I know. In right, out right. I don't know why I can't…

She trips. Her bag flies through the air. Her mother's articles—the inflatable headrest, the underwear and the bodice-ripping novels—spill out over the floor.

Sorry.

GARY *picks up a pair of bloomers.*

GARY: [*holding up the underwear*] Sexy.

SCARLETT *snatches it.*

STEVE: Where have you been?
GARY: Picking up her guide dog.
SCARLETT: I had to get stuff for my mother.

STEVE *picks up a couple of the spilt books.*

STEVE: *Surge of Passion*? *A Woman Has Needs*?
SCARLETT: Her bone mass is very low.
STEVE: Scarlett, how many times have you been on your final warning?
SCARLETT: [*hanging her head*] Quite a few.
STEVE: And how many times have you been on your final, final warning?
SCARLETT: I'll help Gordon clean up out there.

She hurries towards the door.

STEVE: Scarlett! Come over here.

GARY *draws his finger across his neck.* SCARLETT *knows what's coming and tries to delay it by changing the topic.*

SCARLETT: [*picking up the menu*] I think this new menu is just so brave. When some restaurants say they're 'innovative' it's just words, but you try and live up to it. Emu and kangaroo? What's been the response?

GARY: Great, if you're an emu or a kangaroo.

STEVE: Scarlett—

SCARLETT: Those beautiful daughters of yours? How old are they now?

STEVE: Four and six.

SCARLETT: They can speak French and English?

STEVE: Yes.

SCARLETT: [*in a French accent*] 'You know, last night was the most wonderful night of my life.'

STEVE: What?

GORDON: Leslie Caron. *Daddy Long Legs.* 1955.

STEVE: Piss off, Gordon. Scarlett, where is your mind at? It's certainly not here in the Crimson Parrot.

SCARLETT: It is, it is. I'm really, really working on that concentration thing you taught me. [*She starts her concentration exercise.*] Mind on the job, the job, the job. Focus on the job, the job comes first. Stray thoughts are nay thoughts, away thoughts, play thoughts, but play is no way when your mind's on the job.

SHELLEY *re-enters. She takes in* STEVE *and* SCARLETT.

STEVE: Scarlett—I admit that occasionally the right food gets to the right table these days, but people do get that extra little thrill when they look down and see the dish they ordered.

GARY: Don't be a bastard, Steve. Table of two, she has to get it right half the time.

STEVE: I'm paying two waitresses and I'm getting one and a quarter. I know you're trying, Scarlett, but I'm sorry—

SCARLETT: [*desperate*] No! No, Steve! I love this place. If I get run over by a bus, I want my ashes to be scattered around the rubber plant in the entrance.

There's a moment of tension as STEVE *decides.*

STEVE: This is the final, final, final warning. Okay? Now get out there and move the emu!

She nods. Extremely relieved and happy. She beams at him.

SCARLETT: [*as Vivien Leigh*] I've always depended on the kindness of strangers.

GORDON: Vivien Leigh, *A Streetcar Named Desire*, 1951.

She nods at him happily as she grabs menus and heads for the door, colliding with SHELLEY *as she comes in with one of the intact plates. It doesn't stay intact.* STEVE *sinks to his knees, à la Stanley in* A Streetcar Named Desire, *but misquoting Rick from* Casablanca.

STEVE: Off all the lousy restaurants in all the suburbs, in all of Melbourne, she has to work in mine.

On screen, Dooley Wilson, the Casablanca *piano player:*

DOOLEY: [*singing*] For nobody else, gave me a thrill,
    With all your faults, I love you still,
    Had to be you, wonderful you, had to be you…
    'Cause my hair is curly,
    Just because my teeth are pearly…

SCENE THREE: SOME DAY MY PRINCE WILL COME

Four hours later. The work night is over except for the cleaning up.
GORDON *is mopping the floor, singing 'Cheek to Cheek' to himself.*
SCARLETT *enters with the dirty tablecloths.*

SCARLETT: Fred Astaire, *Top Hat*, 1943.

GORDON: Careful, darling, don't kick the—

SCARLETT kicks the bucket, stumbles and falls into the washing basket with the tablecloths.

Are you alright?

SCARLETT gets out of washing basket.

SCARLETT: I'm hopeless at everything, Gordon.

GORDON: Join the club, darling.

SCARLETT: At least you were good at something once.

GORDON: My dear, when the peak of my acting career was playing Mother Goose five times in the Geelong Christmas Pantomime, and a mincing Pirate in an aborted tour of *Penzance*, it's no surprise that kitchen sink drama became my metier. What did you watch last night?

SCARLETT: [*becoming Ingrid Bergman*] Kiss me. Kiss me as if it were the last time.

GORDON: Too easy. [*He becomes Humphrey Bogart.*] We'll always have Paris. We didn't have, we'd lost it, until you came to Casablanca. We got it back last night.

SCARLETT: And I said I'd never leave you.

GORDON: And you never will. But I've got a job to do, too. What I've got to do, you can't be any part of.

> *He picks up his mop and bucket.* SCARLETT *tries to smile through her tears.* GORDON *puts his hand to her chin and raises her face to meet his own.*

Here's lookin' at you, kid.

SCARLETT: Oh, Gordon. Are there men like Humphrey Bogart in the real world?

GORDON: My dear, Humphrey Bogart wasn't like Humphrey Bogart in the real world. He wore a rug and had false teeth. That's why he 'talked like that'.

SCARLETT: Don't you want to share your life with someone?

GORDON: Nobody loves a fairy when she's forty, dear. Well… forty-ish.

SCARLETT: I think I must have the 'Someday My Prince Will Come' gene.

> SCARLETT*'s mind transports her into the shimmering world of 'There Must Be Somebody Waiting for Me (in Loveland)' from the finale of* Glorifying the American Girl *and she sings.*

SCENE FOUR: SPEED DATING

Later that night. SCARLETT *comes in carrying the bag full of her mother's requests. She puts them down and sits… on the TV remote. Ad for lonely hearts.* SCARLETT *switches it off and slumps.* MAUREEN *enters.*

MAUREEN: I thought you'd never get home.
SCARLETT: Why are you still up?
MAUREEN: My friend Eileen rang.
SCARLETT: So?

ACT ONE 17

MAUREEN: Well, you know how her daughter Leanne was having no luck at all finding a partner.
SCARLETT: Why don't I find that surprising?
MAUREEN: Alright. She's not the sort of woman who attracts men at first glance.
SCARLETT: Or second or third…
MAUREEN: But she has a go-getting personality.
SCARLETT: That's an understatement.
MAUREEN: Alright. Don't listen. But she's planning a wedding and you're not.
SCARLETT: Who is she marrying?
MAUREEN: He's not conventionally good-looking—
SCARLETT: Oh, the Elephant Man…
MAUREEN: —and he's a little overweight.
SCARLETT: Orca, the great white whale…
MAUREEN: Oh yes, make fun of me. But beggars can't be choosers, you know.
SCARLETT: Mum…
MAUREEN: You could've been married to Roger by now, and I could have—
SCARLETT: Mum, Roger—let's not go there.
MAUREEN: He wasn't an outgoing personality, I'll grant you that— but fully qualified horticulturalists don't grow on trees.
SCARLETT: Mum, he sniffed. And said y'know. [*Imitating him*] 'Scarlett, y'know, [*sniff*] I've been thinking y'know, [*sniff*] that y'know, [*sniff*] your first grandchild?' [*Imitating her mother as a doting grandparent*] 'Hello, little Sinus.'
MAUREEN: Leanne's a night nurse. Same problem with hours as you. Do you want to know how she met him, or do you not?
SCARLETT: I do not.
MAUREEN: She found out about 'Love in the Morning'. They run speed-dating breakfasts for shiftworkers.
SCARLETT: Mum! No!
MAUREEN: Why?
SCARLETT: Because there is this thing called dignity. And I still have some.
MAUREEN: Dignity is a luxury you can't afford to have at your age. It's so frustrating, Scarlett. You could have had Vera's son. Just back from New York, divorced, lonely, disorientated—he would have

said yes to anyone, but no, you let that vulture Valerie get to him first, and it was all over, red rover.
SCARLETT: I don't want to 'grab' someone lonely and disorientated.
MAUREEN: Alright. End your life a lonely bitter spinster. What do you think my life would have been without you?

> MAUREEN *storms off to bed.*

SCARLETT: [*to her departing mother*] A lot more active. [*She throws her mother's inflatable headrest at the door.*] You'd have to get these yourself. [*And the books and the bloomers.*] I want someone who sees me across a crowded room and loves me.

> *On screen, Anna Karenina's famous first encounter with Vronsky at the train station transports* SCARLETT *to the world of her dreams. Greta Garbo morphs into Scarlett.*
>
> *At the end of the film segment Anna (*SCARLETT*) looks away.*

SCENE FIVE: ROO SELLS AND STEVE EXCELS

Next day, 8.00 p.m. We're in the restaurant. There's action in the kitchen as STEVE *and* GARY *work on the orders.*

GARY: Table Fourteen, good to go. One bug tail, one barra, one beef burger and a beer battered bream.
STEVE: Scarlett! Will you help Shelley?! Scarlett!
GARY: Shel can handle four at once, can't you, Shel?
SHELLEY: [*smiling sweetly*] Gary, can you still speak Greek?
GARY: Yeah, sure.
SHELLEY: *Malaka!*

> GARY *is speechless, deeply wounded.*

GORDON: What's that mean?
GARY: Gordon. Don't go there.
STEVE: [*taking the next order chit down*] I don't believe it! Who ordered the emu and the kangaroo?
SHELLEY: It certainly wasn't me.
STEVE: Scarlett? Amazing. [*Remembering*] Shit! Emu leg's in the deep freeze.
GARY: I'll hack a chunk off and whack it in the microwave.

ACT ONE

As GARY opens the coolroom door there's a crash and SCARLETT emerges with a bag of ice, limping.

SCARLETT: Sorry, Gary.

  STEVE *comes across to* SCARLETT, *the order chit in his hands, looking delighted.*

STEVE: Hey!—You sold the emu and the kangaroo?

SCARLETT: No, they wanted it. They said it was more environmentally friendly.

STEVE: Yeah?

SCARLETT: They told me that to get a kilo of rump steak on the table takes fifty thousand litres of water. And puts five hundred kilograms of carbon into the atmosphere?

STEVE: Five hundred kilograms?

SCARLETT: Maybe it was fifty. Whatever it was was still scary.

GARY: All that environment stuff is bullshit.

GORDON: So what's melting the polar caps? Whale piss?

GARY: What would you know, you fucking old leftie poof?

SCARLETT: Gary.

STEVE: Put a sock in it, you two!

GARY: I wouldn't let him wash our dishes. Who knows where his fingers have been?

GORDON: Gary, you know perfectly well I always wash my hands after I've jerked you off.

GARY: [*disgusted*] That is offensive, you fuckin' ass-bandit!

SCARLETT: Steve, you shouldn't let him say that stuff.

STEVE: Yeah, stop baiting him, Gordon.

SCARLETT: [*horrified*] Not Gordon—

GARY: Fucking political correctness. A poof is a poof, you're contravening my civil rights if I can't say so!

GORDON: That suspended sentence for sex with a fifteen-year-old, Gary? Was it two years or three?

GARY: Aw yeah, very funny…

SCARLETT: [*singing*] 'Thank heaven for little girls…'

GARY: Fuck off.

SCARLETT & GORDON: [*together*] Maurice Chevalier. *Gigi*. 1958.
  [*Singing*] '… for little girls grow bigger every day…'

SHELLEY, who entered the kitchen during the last part of the performance, tosses her head contemptuously.

SHELLEY: One day you guys will watch a film where the actors on screen are still alive.

STEVE: [*putting out four plates*] Table Twelve, good to go. Hot.

SHELLEY moves to get them.

Scarlett! Will you help Shelley and grab those other two plates? I am still praying for that groundbreaking moment when a table of four actually get their mains together.

GARY: [*yelling frantically*] Hot!

Too late. SCARLETT *has already picked up the plate and yells.* GORDON *grabs it before it falls, but now his fingers are burning and he yells.*

He passes the plates to GARY *and plunges his hands in the sink.* GARY *yells and hands the plates to* STEVE. SCARLETT *grabs two napkins and retrieves the plates.*

SCARLETT: Sorry, Gordon. Sorry, Gary. Sorry, Steve.

SCARLETT *takes the two plates and exits.*

GARY: She's bloody hopeless. Should've got rid of her by now.

STEVE: She's on her final warning.

GARY: Too soft, mate. When I have my restaurant it's my way or the highway.

GORDON: The customers love her. Even when she gives them the wrong order.

STEVE: I can't for the love of me see why.

GORDON: Every now and then you get a freak of nature. No envy, no malice…

STEVE: No hand-eye co-ordination, no concentration span, no short-term memory, no long-term memory…

GARY: Except for films shot seventy years ago.

He stares at something GARY *is cooking.*

STEVE: Gary!

GARY *notices he's been cooking something on the hotplate for too long.*

GARY: Gawd, sorry boss.

Bob Horney as Gordon, Caroline O'Connor as Scarlett, Marney McQueen as Shelley, Andrew McFarlane as Steve and Simon Wood as Gary in the 2008 MTC production. (Photo: Jeff Busby)

STEVE: [*sarcastically*] No, no. Your way's better. Only an old has-been like me would leave in the flavour and moisture. Burn it some more.

> *Outside in the restaurant* SHELLEY *and* SCARLETT *have delivered the dishes to Table Twelve which is out of sight. There's the sound of raucous laughter offstage.* SCARLETT *comes back into the kitchen looking upset.* GORDON *looks at her.*

GORDON: What's wrong?
SCARLETT: It's fine.
GORDON: Did those yobbos on Table Nine say something?
GARY: Yobbos? Do yous know who they are?
GORDON: Rocket scientists?
GARY: That's Stu Dundell, Wayne Mutton, Denton Slade and Clinton Zlitsky.
GORDON: And who exactly are they?
GARY: You freakin' old queen. They're the greatest midfield in the history of footy. Stu Dundell is probably the best footballer who ever pulled on boots.
GORDON: I bet that's not all he's pulled on.
GARY: Stu never wanked in his life, you old poof. He's the king of freakin' Beaver Palace.
STEVE: [*to* SCARLETT, *seeing she's still upset*] Did those dropkicks give you a hard time?
SCARLETT: It's fine.
STEVE: [*not believing her*] Scarlett.
SCARLETT: It's fine.

> SHELLEY *sweeps into the kitchen looking pleased with herself. She smiles condescendingly to* SCARLETT.

SHELLEY: Don't take it personally.
STEVE: What?
SHELLEY: The guys on Table Nine. [*To* SCARLETT] They shouldn't have said that to you, but you know… [*with a shrug*] guys.
GARY: What did they say?
SHELLEY: That Scarlett would get bigger tips with implants.
GARY: [*to* SCARLETT] Worth thinking about.
STEVE: Right. That's it. They're out.
GARY: You're kidding. Having Stu Dundell out there is gold.
STEVE: No-one talks to my staff like that.

ACT ONE

He strides to the door angrily and crosses the restaurant. SCARLETT *walks out after him and watches as he goes offstage. The situation triggers a film sequence in* SCARLETT*'s head. It's the classic scene from* Tarzan *in which the hero protects Jane from marauding lions. The screen heroes morph into Scarlett and Steve.*

Back in the restaurant STEVE *strides past into the kitchen.*

Arseholes. Right, let's get back to work. There's a cover waiting in the banquette. Scarlett?

SCARLETT: Yes, yes of course, Steve…

She goes out to the banquette, still distracted by STEVE*'s show of valour. The guy waiting is jumpy, anxious, nervous.*

Hi, I'm Scarlett. I'll be your waitress tonight. Had a good day?

ALAN: Ah, yes, well ah—

She picks up the napkin to shake it loose so she can put it in his lap and nearly flicks his eye out in the process.

SCARLETT: Sorry. Sorry.

She drops the menu. The both reach for it at once and knock heads.

Sorry. The menu.

ALAN: Thanks. [*Looking at the menu*] Strange name.

SCARLETT: My mother loved *Gone with the Wind* .

ALAN: Sorry?

SCARLETT: Scarlett O'Hara in *Gone*—

ALAN: Oh. No. No, no. Not Scarlett. No, the Crimson Parrot.

SCARLETT: Oh. Yes.

ALAN: Why the Crimson Parrot?

SCARLETT: Seen *Casablanca*?

ALAN: I think so. Humphrey Bogart?

SCARLETT: [*nodding*] And Ingrid Bergman. Greatest love story ever filmed.

ALAN: [*nodding*] Rick's bar. 'Play it again, Sam.'

SCARLETT: The actual quote is: 'Play it, Sam. Play "As Time Goes By".'

ALAN: Right, I'll work on that.

SCARLETT: The rival restaurant to Rick's in *Casablanca* is the Blue Parrot.

ALAN: Ah, right.

SCARLETT: When our owner Steve wanted to change our name I suggested it, but Steve wanted it to sound more Australian so he called it the Crimson Parrot.

ALAN: But everything's green.

SCARLETT: Steve said Crimson looked too Chinese.

ALAN: I'm not sure you ended up with the right name.

SCARLETT: No.

ALAN: I think Scarlett's a nice name.

SCARLETT: Yeah, but Scarlett O'Hara?

ALAN: O'Hara?

SCARLETT: [*nodding her head*] It's as bad as if a Mrs Bush called her kid George.

ALAN: [*puzzled*] She did.

SCARLETT: No, another Mrs Bush… [*She decides she'll let that one go.*] What I was going to say is that it didn't need to happen because my name's really Smeaton. My father was an O'Hara, but he never married my mother. Actually the truth is he left her before I was born. My mother called us O'Hara because she thought it was more respectable. The logic kind of escapes me, but there you go. Look, you don't want to hear all of this. You're probably really hungry and thinking 'When is she ever going to shut up and take my order?'

ALAN: No, no.

SCARLETT: [*fetching the water jug*] Steve, the boss here, thinks I'm a bit away with the fairies so I'm really working to try and stay more focused.

ALAN: Ah…

She pours the water.

SCARLETT: Perhaps you'd like to hear our specials. The chargrilled kangaroo sirloin with ah, ah, some sort of chilli thing… on top. And emu fillet with with… er… jew stuff. A real customer favourite that one. Very, very good.

ALAN: Ah, look… maybe not.

He scours the menu. She waits, but silences make her nervous.

SCARLETT: You won't find a menu quite like this anywhere else in the country. Our chef's very innovative. We had crocodile and cumquat ragout a few weeks back. Didn't catch on. Anything rocking your boat?

ALAN: Ah. No.

He stares at the menu. There's another silence.

SCARLETT: If the emu isn't your cup of tea, I'd highly recommend the chargrilled kangaroo sirloin.

ALAN: What about the rib eye steak. That looks nice?

SCARLETT: Fine. [*Beat.*] Fine. Although I have to say I was really worried the other day when I heard it takes fifty thousand litres of water to get a kilo of beef steak on the table.

ALAN: Yes, well—

SCARLETT: Interestingly enough, kangaroo takes less than a thousand. And basically it's far healthier. Almost zero saturated fat. But don't think I'm trying to push you into something you don't want. The beef steak?

> ALAN *stares at her and nods, then he stares at the menu, then stares at her again. He has a panic attack, immobilised by the fact that he can't order kangaroo, when he knows he's supposed to.*

I'll get you some bread.

> *She turns away and he uses the opportunity to get up and leave at high speed without even looking back.* SCARLETT *turns back and finds him gone.*
>
> *Meanwhile, back in the kitchen...*

SHELLEY: Stu Dundell asked me for my phone number.

GARY: He won't call.

SHELLEY: Wanna bet?

GORDON: What about your boyfriend?

SHELLEY: Gordon, Stu Dundell?!

GORDON: Aren't you engaged?

> SCARLETT *picks up* ALAN*'s menu and takes it to the kitchen.*

GARY: Starfucker.

SHELLEY: Look at my finger, Gary. Do you see an engagement ring on there? No. Derek's dragon of a mother thinks I'm not good enough for him because I didn't go to Tintern Girls Grammar and learn to go through life without farting.

GARY: Derek told me you give great head. Most mothers would be pleased.

> SHELLEY, *plates in her hands, sweeps out disdainfully.*

STEVE: What did the guy in the banquette order?

SCARLETT: [*looking shamefaced*] He left.
STEVE: He left? Why?
SCARLETT: I don't know. We seemed to be getting on really well.
STEVE: He just left?

>   *She nods sadly.*

There's a party of four just come in on Ten. See if you can perhaps convince them to stay. I make a little more money that way.
SCARLETT: Steve?
STEVE: Yes?
SCARLETT: Thank you for… dealing with those footballers.
STEVE: You don't get paid enough to cop that kind of humiliation.

>   STEVE *exits to his office with* SCARLETT *staring after him. On the screen,* SCARLETT *claws across rocks to* STEVE *to embrace him, as in* Duel in the Sun.

SCARLETT: I love you.
STEVE: Don't cry, honey. Don't cry.
SCARLETT: I had to do it, Steve. I had to do it.
STEVE: Of course you did. Let me… let me hold you.
SCARLETT: Yes. Hold me. Hold me once, Steve.
STEVE: Little… butterfingers.

>   STEVE *sees that she's still standing there.*

Are you okay?
SCARLETT: [*snapping out of it*] Oh. Fine. Sorry, sorry.

>   *Embarrassed, she hurries out into the restaurant.*
>
>   *On the screen, a sperm wriggles enthusiastically towards an egg.*

SCENE SIX: SPERM BANKS

Sunday night, 8.25 p.m. MAUREEN *is watching a television documentary on sperm donors. When* SCARLETT *comes in she's watching a particularly emotional moment in which a mother is crying her eyes out on learning that she's finally become pregnant.*

SCARLETT: Mum, what's wrong? What is it, Mum? Mum, tell me…
MAUREEN: [*pointing at the TV*] A very moving documentary from America. Look, Scarlett, this could be the answer to our prayers.

SCARLETT: What?
MAUREEN: She's been trying to have a baby for six years. She chose a father from a sperm bank.
SCARLETT: Sperm bank! Mum…
MAUREEN: You can choose any sperm you like. Tall, short, arty, athletic, intellectual. She chose a Nobel Prize winner. Look how happy she is, Scarlett. I've been crying almost since it started.
SCARLETT: Mum, it's not an option, right?
MAUREEN: Wouldn't you like a child whose father was a Nobel Prize winner?
SCARLETT: And help him with his preschool quantum physics assignments?
MAUREEN: Or a basketballer. They make a fortune.

    SCARLETT *mimes talking to a very tall child.*

SCARLETT: Hello, little Shaq. Did you dig in the sandpit again today?
MAUREEN: You'd get a damn sight better genes than you seem to be able to organise on your own account! You can even do it yourself, Scarlett. They showed you, all you need is one of these. [*Producing a turkey baster*] I had one in the kitchen. I only use it at Christmas.
SCARLETT: Mum, the only sperm donor I want is called a husband.

    MAUREEN *sighs.* SCARLETT *starts to unpack the leftovers she's brought home from the restaurant.*

MAUREEN: Aren't there any nice men who come to the restaurant?
SCARLETT: The restaurant? Well, there's currently a man who runs every time he sees me, and there's one very butch lesbian in leather who's showing some interest, but no. Mum, it's not going to happen. Get used to it. Do you want a yam vol au vent?
MAUREEN: Sounds disgusting. It's a wonder you get any customers.
SCARLETT: No more Discovery Channel. Let's see what's on TCM.

    SCARLETT *takes up the remote control and switches the cable channel. It's* Calamity Jane, *the famous romantic scene in which Calamity Jane realises she loves Wild Bill Hickok. They are sitting side by side in the moonlight.*

CALAMITY: [*on screen*] Oh, Bill. All I've done for months is dream about him. About getting married and building a cabin… and having young'uns.

    MAUREEN *looks at* SCARLETT *meaningfully.* SCARLETT *bridles.*

I know it sounds silly, I guess, but... Oh, Bill, I really wanted all those things.

BILL: [*on screen*] I was kinda hankering for them myself.

SCARLETT, the romantic junkie, is by now engrossed, with her vol au vent suspended on its way to her mouth.

CALAMITY: [*on screen*] There'll never be another man like him. Not for me. Not ever.

BILL: [*on screen*] It ain't going to be easy getting her outa my system either. She was so beautiful and...

They kiss...

Oh, Bill.

On screen Calamity and Wild Bill look into each other's eyes and slowly realise they don't love the people they've been talking about, but each other. They draw closer and kiss.

SCENE SEVEN: ALAN RUNS AGAIN

Next day, 7.50 p.m. The restaurant. Frantic activity in the kitchen.

STEVE: Scarlett!

He gives her a cheese grater.

Make yourself useful. Prep the parmesan for the yabby ravioli.

As STEVE *draws close he triggers thoughts of Howard Keel from the* Calamity Jane *movie scene she saw last night. Up on the screen* STEVE *becomes Howard Keel with his cheesy grin and* SCARLETT *becomes Calamity.*

BILL/STEVE: [*on screen*] It ain't going to be easy getting her outa my system either. She was so beautiful and...

They kiss.

CALAMITY/SCARLETT: Oh, Steve. Oh, Steve.

On screen SCARLETT *and* STEVE *look into each other's eyes and kiss. Absorbed in her fantasy,* SCARLETT *hugs the cheese grater and yells.*

STEVE: Scarlett, mind on the job!

SHELLEY *enters.*

ACT ONE

And where the hell have you been?
SHELLEY: Table Six. They're still deciding.
STEVE: Still?
SHELLEY: They're foodies. Some of them think the quandong chilli glaze is a little pretentious.
STEVE: And the others?
SHELLEY: They think it's a total wank.
STEVE: [*outraged*] I spent weeks perfecting that.

He moves towards the door, but GORDON *plants himself in the way.*

GORDON: Chef. I love it when you're butch, but last time you debated food with customers, the local paper called it restaurant rage.
STEVE: Everyone who can put a pan over a flame thinks they're a freakin' foodie!

He tries to move out but GORDON *continues to hold onto him and, looking into his eyes, impersonates the husky voice of the sexy young Lauren Bacall.*

GORDON: [*as Bacall, to* STEVE] You know, Steve. You don't have to say anything and you don't have to do anything. Oh, maybe just whistle. You know how to whistle, don't ya, Steve? You just put your lips together and blow.

SCARLETT *joins in for* 'You just put your lips together and blow'.

SCARLETT: Lauren Bacall. *To Have and Have Not*, 1944.
STEVE: [*shaking his head at the two of them*] I just wish you two would occasionally try and live in the real world.

But the diversion has diffused STEVE'*s anger and he returns to his station.* SHELLEY *sweeps in.*

SHELLEY: Weirdo alert. Desperate and dateless at the banquette. You deal with him, Scarlett. A party of six has just come in.
STEVE: [*to* SCARLETT] Try and move the buffalo casserole. It's on its last legs.
GARY: Its legs have been pointing to the sky for three days.
STEVE: [*shouting*] It's just reached its peak.

SHELLEY *sweeps out into the restaurant.* SCARLETT *follows her.* ALAN *is sitting there at the same banquette. He's tried to disguise himself in a beanie and dark glasses.*

SCARLETT: Hi, my name is Scarlett, I'll be your...

She tries to pick up his napkin but he grabs it, anxious to avoid a repeat of last night's incident. After a brief struggle, his disguise comes off.

Oh, hello! Weren't you here the other night?

ALAN: Er... was I?

SCARLETT: Did something I do upset you?

ALAN: No, no. [*He holds up a BlackBerry.*] Something cropped up. Got buzzed. Had to go.

SCARLETT: I thought it was maybe because of the stuff I said.

ALAN: No.

SCARLETT: I mean that was true about the fifty thousand litres of water per kilo of steak, but I shouldn't have—

ALAN: No. [*He holds up the BlackBerry.*] No, message. Had to go.

SCARLETT: Are you an obstetrician?

ALAN: No.

SCARLETT: Most people who get paged are obstetricians. My mother said I was an obstetrician's nightmare. I was in breach position, and every time he tried to turn me round I just went back again. Then the cord got caught around my throat and my heartbeat was getting weaker and weaker. Talk about panic. It was seventy-eight hours from the time her water broke. And when I finally came out my face was blue, they couldn't get me to breathe. I had mucus blocking all the airways, dripping everywhere. What would you like to eat?

ALAN: [*has been put off eating*] Ah...

SCARLETT: A drink to start?

ALAN: [*grateful for the suggestion*] Ah, yes.

SCARLETT: The wine list's there.

As she points at the menu, SCARLETT *falls on to* ALAN, *injuring his groin and getting caught up in the tablecloth. As she frees herself,* ALAN, *using the menu as protection, points randomly.*

ALAN: I'll have a bottle of that.

SCARLETT *stares at the menu in disbelief.*

SCARLETT: You're sure?

ALAN: It's no good?

ACT ONE

SCARLETT: No... Good. It's just we don't often sell the Grange Hermitage '89. [*She runs into the kitchen, dropping* ALAN*'s menu.*] He's ordered the Grange Hermitage.

SHELLEY: [*suddenly interested*] Grange Hermitage? Eight hundred dollars a bottle?

> *Out in the restaurant* ALAN *overhears the drama and creeps towards his fallen menu to check the price.*

STEVE: We haven't got Grange Hermitage.

GARY: It's just there to make the list look good.

SHELLEY: He must be loaded.

SCARLETT: What do I do?

STEVE: Tell him we just sold our last bottle. Steer him towards the Rawson's Retreat.

SCARLETT: When he wants Grange Hermitage?

STEVE: Same grape.

> SCARLETT *goes to the wine rack for Rawson's Retreat.* SHELLEY *blocks her way and snatches the bottle.*

SHELLEY: I'll take it to him.

> SCARLETT *snatches the bottle back.*

SCARLETT: I thought you were saving yourself for Stu Dumbell.

SHELLEY: Dundell, dingbat. Don't you know anything?

> SCARLETT *heads for the swinging doors as* STEVE *goes to his office.*

STEVE: Don't forget the buffalo casserole.

GORDON: Those who've tasted it will never forget the buffalo casserole.

> SCARLETT *comes out to the banquette to find* ALAN *gone. She goes back into the kitchen.*

SCARLETT: He's gone again.

GARY: You're kidding me? A guy who can afford Grange freakin' Hermitage, you handcuff him to the freakin' table.

SHELLEY: I told you I should have taken it.

SCARLETT: He just left.

> SHELLEY*'s mobile phone rings in her bag. She answers it.*

GARY: If it ever makes that noise again I'll drown it in the frig'n soup.

SHELLEY: [*on the mobile, imperiously*] Yes. [*A sudden change of tone*] Stu, how nice of you to ring. Stu, how absolutely wonderful to hear from you.

> *The rest of them look at each other.*

Stu, what a great idea. I love to dance. Love it. Oh, and Stu, marvellous game last week. [*Pause.*] Ankle injury. Oh, of course. I meant the week before. It's amazing that I should bump into you. I've been a Kangaroo supporter since I was tiny. [*Pause.*] Your stripes go the other way? Sorry. I'll text you my address. [*She smiles, nods and turns triumphantly to them, putting her mobile back in her bag.*] That, just happened to be Stu Dundell.

SCARLETT: We kind of worked that out.

SHELLEY: We're going out for dinner.

GORDON: Mama, face it. I was the slut of all time

SCARLETT: Elizabeth Taylor, *Butterfield 8*, 1960.

> SHELLEY *looks at them all again, triumphantly, then sweeps out.*
> GARY *goes and gets* SHELLEY's *mobile from her bag.*

GARY: What's her boyfriend's name?

SCARLETT: [*exiting to the coolroom*] Derek.

GARY: Derek.

> GARY *wipes his hands and moves to the lockers shiftily.*

GORDON: Gary, what are you up to?

GARY: Never you mind. Little Miss Slut-Features has to face the music sometime.

> *On screen: 'Let's Face the Music and Dance' from* Follow the Fleet. *Fred and Ginger dance and a curtain closes on them.*

SCENE EIGHT: ADIEU MADELEINE

Three hours later. STEVE *is sitting alone at the banquette, drinking white wine.* SCARLETT *is leaving in her bike helmet and sees* STEVE *looking melancholy.*

SCARLETT: 'Night, Steve.

STEVE: 'Night.

> SCARLETT *looks back at* STEVE. *Her imagination sees him as Rick in* Casablanca, *sitting lonely in the bar. She edges back towards him.*

ACT ONE

SCARLETT: Great night for the planet.

STEVE: Mmm. What?

SCARLETT: I sold eight portions of kangaroo, and four emu. Did you notice? I told them about the five hundred kilos of carbon and they switched to the roo. The environmental thing is getting really big. My cousin Carmen brought one of those hybrid cars, except it knocked this old lady over because you can't hear them coming. Everything she does she buys a carbon offset. What's a carbon offset?

STEVE: If you take a plane you plant some trees.

SCARLETT: Our body corporate won't let us plant a thing.

STEVE: No, somebody else does it for you.

SCARLETT: That's really nice.

STEVE: I'd better go.

SCARLETT: Home to Madeleine?

STEVE: No, Madeleine is in Paris with the two kids.

SCARLETT: How nice. Gone to meet their grandpère and grandmère?

STEVE looks at her.

No?

STEVE: Forget it. I didn't mean to talk about it.

There's a silence. STEVE looks at SCARLETT. He knows she's the most sympathetic ear around, and he does want to unburden himself to someone.

She made it clear she doesn't want me to be part of her life any longer.

SCARLETT stares at him.

SCARLETT: No.

STEVE: I should've seen it coming.

SCARLETT: I thought things were fine.

STEVE: She's an ex-fashion model, Parisian to the core, and what am I? The owner of a restaurant called the Crimson Parrot that's bleeding money.

SCARLETT: If you love someone you stick with them through thick and thin.

STEVE: If that's true, the laws of logic allow only one conclusion.

This leaves SCARLETT with nothing to say.

SCARLETT: When did she go?

STEVE: A week ago. Don't tell anyone else. You're the only person I feel I can trust.

> *Suddenly* SCARLETT*'s film imagination takes over. She is Ingrid Bergman and* STEVE *is Humphrey Bogart. She lifts her face to his. He kisses her gently.*

INGRID: Kiss me. Kiss me as if it were the last time.

> *They kiss tenderly. On the film image a glass is knocked over.* SCARLETT, *still in the fantasy, approaches* STEVE *to do likewise. She snaps out of her reverie and leaps back feeling guilty and spills wine from a glass onto* STEVE*'s lap.*

SCARLETT: Steve, I'm so sorry. How are you coping?

STEVE: Not so good. The truth is I'm a wreck. I promised her I'd have a chain of restaurants in a few years. Just be the Executive Chef and leave it to the others to do the work. Travel the world. Three months a year in France. Big joke. I've only kept the door open here because my bank manager enjoys watching me crawl to his desk on my belly.

SCARLETT: It's that bad?

STEVE: It's that bad.

SCARLETT: You're a very good chef.

STEVE: Do you know the worst fate anyone can have? To be very good at something but not very, very good.

SCARLETT: [*shaking her head*] I'd settle for quite good… at anything.

STEVE: People like you, Scarlett. That's worth a lot.

> SCARLETT *finds herself being drawn to him again…*

> STEVE *is Humphrey and* SCARLETT *Ingrid as he chucks her under the chin in the last scene of* Casablanca.

STEVE/HUMPHREY: Now, now. Here's looking at you, kid.

STEVE: See you tomorrow.

> STEVE *exits to his office. Back up on screen, Doris Day rides into shot and begins the famous song 'Secret Love' from* Calamity Jane. *She quickly morphs into Scarlett.*

SCARLETT: Once I had a secret love,
    That lived within the heart of me.
    All too soon my secret love,
    Became impatient to be free.

Now I shout it from the highest hill,
Even told the golden daffodils,
At last my heart's an open door,
And my secret love's not secret anymore.

SCENE NINE: IN LOVE

Later that night. SCARLETT *sits on the couch in her apartment, staring at the walls.* MAUREEN *comes out of her bedroom looking concerned.*

MAUREEN: Sweetie. What are you doing?
SCARLETT: Nothing.
MAUREEN: Why aren't you watching one of your videos?
SCARLETT: Mum.
MAUREEN: What?

> MAUREEN *senses from her daughter's expression that something is troubling her. She sits down beside her and waits.*

SCARLETT: I think I've fallen in love.

> MAUREEN *stares at her, delighted.*

MAUREEN: Thank God. Don't take offence, dear, but frankly your biological clock is at three minutes to midnight. Tell me about him.

> SCARLETT *looks woebegone.* MAUREEN *becomes suspicious.*

SCARLETT: I can't.
MAUREEN: Why not? Is there some… problem with him?

> SCARLETT *shakes her head.*

He's not a bikie?

> SCARLETT *shakes her head.*

A criminal with tattoos?

> SCARLETT *shakes her head.*

[*A terrible thought hits her*] He's not… Lebanese?

> SCARLETT *bites her lip to hold back the tears and shakes her head.*

SCARLETT: He's married. With children.
MAUREEN: Scarlett darling. This is not good. Not good.
SCARLETT: His wife's left him and taken the kids.

Monica Maughan as Maureen and Caroline O'Connor as Scarlett in the 2008 MTC production. (Photo: Jeff Busby)

MAUREEN: She'll come back and all you'll be left with is a broken heart. Look at what happened to me with Ron Standish. You remember him?
SCARLETT: No.
MAUREEN: You were only three or four. He had the Ford dealership in Koo Wee Rup. Swore he was going to leave his wife and kids, but never had the slightest intention.
SCARLETT: I remember the carpet layer. He certainly lived up to his vocation. Wasn't he married too?
MAUREEN: Darling, when you're lumbered with a child, they're all married. All except Father Carmichael.
SCARLETT: Father Carmichael. You didn't have an affair with Father Carmichael?
MAUREEN: Not really an affair but perhaps a little more than pastoral comfort. But then they made him choirmaster and he got too busy. It never works, darling. Take my advice and break this off immediately.
SCARLETT: Mum, he's not the slightest bit interested in me. His wife was on the cover of *Vogue*.
MAUREEN: When they've had a shock, they'll clutch at anything.
SCARLETT: Thank you very much.
MAUREEN: Darling, I didn't mean it like that, but you'd be the first to agree you're not likely to make the cover of *Vogue*.
SCARLETT: I have reluctantly accepted that possibility.
MAUREEN: I know I shouldn't keep putting all this pressure on you. It's just that I want to see you in a beautiful house with a lovely man, your own children and a granny flat out the back for me. This thing is just a temporary infatuation.
SCARLETT: No, it isn't, Mum. It isn't.
MAUREEN: Alright, but don't say I didn't warn you.
SCARLETT: You can't control your heart.

> SCARLETT's *film imagination clicks into* Gone with the Wind, *with* STEVE *as Trevor Howard and her as Vivien Leigh.*

STEVE: What is it, Scarlett? A secret? Who are you hiding from in here?
SCARLETT: Oh, Steve, Steve. I love you.
STEVE: Scarlett.
SCARLETT: I love you, I do. Have I your heart, my darling? I love you. I love you.

STEVE: You mustn't say such things. You're so young and unthinking, you don't know what marriage means.
SCARLETT: I know I love you and I want to be your wife. You don't love Madeleine.
STEVE: She's like me, Scarlett. She's part of my blood. We understand each other.
SCARLETT: But you love me!

SCENE TEN: ALAN'S RISE, SHELLEY'S FALL, STEVE'S IDEA

Three days later, 7.39 p.m. In the restaurant, the night's work is underway. It hasn't reached a frantic level in the kitchen yet as it's early. GORDON *is holding a carrot.*

GORDON: 'As God is my witness, I'll never go hungry again.'
STEVE: Gordon, can you stop all that shit and get on with it!
GARY: Bloody necrofilmiac.
STEVE: [*to* GORDON] Specials for tonight. The specials tonight are emu samosas and buffalo vindaloo.
GARY: Got to use that shit up somehow.

    GORDON *exits.*

STEVE: Jesus, Gary, am I the only person who takes this business seriously?
GARY: Okay, okay, keep your hair on.

    GARY *goes out to the coolroom.*

STEVE: Things are on a knife edge.
SCARLETT: Are things really that bad?
STEVE. It's crunch time.
SCARLETT: Steve, I'm really sorry. I'll try and move the vindaloo.
STEVE: I appreciate that, Scarlett. You might make mistakes but deep down I know you care.
SCARLETT: [*blushing*] Thanks, Steve. I lay awake last night thinking about… what you told me. It's just so awful.
STEVE: A postcard arrived today. I thought 'She's come to her senses'. Do you know what it said?

    SCARLETT *shakes her head vigorously.*

    'Je suis desolé que je ne t'aime plus, mais j'adore Paris.'

ACT ONE

SCARLETT *waits for the translation.*

SCARLETT: What does that mean?

STEVE: I'm sorry. I don't love you anymore, but I adore Paris.

SCARLETT: [*reaching out to touch him*] Steve, that's awful.

> *But the intimate moment is disrupted by the arrival back of both* GORDON *and* GARY.

GORDON: Scarlett, our galloping gourmet is back. He asked especially for you.

STEVE: Tell him if he runs again I'll catch him, bring him back and staple his friggin' balls to the banquette.

> STEVE *exits to his office with* SCARLETT *staring after him. On screen,* SCARLETT *claws across rocks to* STEVE *to embrace him, as in* Duel in the Sun.

SCARLETT: I love you.

STEVE: Don't cry, honey. Don't cry.

SCARLETT: I had to do it, Steve. I had to do it.

STEVE: Of course you did. Let me... let me hold you.

SCARLETT: Yes. Hold me. Hold me once, Steve.

STEVE: Little... butterfingers.

GORDON: Penne for your thoughts.

> *She sees* GORDON *looking at her, puzzled, and snaps out of it. She goes into the restaurant to see* ALAN.

SCARLETT: You sure you don't want to save us both the trouble and walk out now?

ALAN: [*tense, edgy*] I'm sorry.

SCARLETT: If there's something I've been doing wrong, please tell me.

ALAN: No, it's not your fault. [*A painful admission*] I didn't read the price.

SCARLETT: We didn't have it, in any case.

> SCARLETT *gives him the menu. He takes it and looks around the restaurant. He's still very nervous.*

ALAN: I came early in the hope...

SCARLETT: In the hope of what?

ALAN: I heard a joke the other day. Would you like to hear it?

SCARLETT: What's your name?

ALAN: Alan.

SCARLETT: You're not Alan Carr the comedian?

ALAN: No, no, I work in IT. I give technical support to the other technical support guys who get stumped.

SCARLETT: You ring them up?

ALAN: No, no. We just type stuff. They're all in India, so I don't get out much. Except sometimes I go to see my grandmother.

SCARLETT: What about your mum and dad?

ALAN: They died when I was young and she brought me up.

SCARLETT: How'd they die?

ALAN: Semi-trailer hit their car. Would you like to hear the joke?

SCARLETT: [*struggling to change gears*] Sure.

>*She sits down.*

ALAN: Well, it's a blonde joke. Oh, I forgot. [*Indicating the kitchen*] The other waitress is blonde.

SCARLETT: Go right ahead.

ALAN: There's this blonde lady training for parachute jumping. The instructor tells her to make sure she pulls the cord by three hundred feet. She says how do I know when it's three hundred feet. He says it's the height where you can recognise people's faces. So she says, ummm. So she says, ummm…

>*He's forgotten. The tension is too great for* SCARLETT. *She finishes it for him.*

SCARLETT: 'What happens if I don't know anyone when I get there?'

>ALAN *looks crestfallen.*

ALAN: I can't believe I forgot the punchline.

SCARLETT: As the great film director Preston Sturges said, a joke without a punchline is like sex without an… It is pretty important.

ALAN: Yeah, right.

>ALAN *stands to run.* SCARLETT*'s onto him.*

SCARLETT: [*severely, as to a dog*] Alan! Alan! Sit!

>ALAN *sits. Hesitates.*

[*Warning*] Stay… Good boy.

>*She passes him the menu.* ALAN *looks at it.*

ALAN: Right… um… What can you, er, tell me about… the chicken?

SCARLETT: The chicken. Very, very good. I took some to my mother and she's the pickiest person in the world and she loved it.
ALAN: [*being bold*] Then let's do the chicken.
SCARLETT: Good choice.
ALAN: And let's have some… wine.
SCARLETT: Why not?
ALAN: A glass of… [*badly mispronounced*] semillon.
SCARLETT: [*pronouncing it correctly*] Semillon?
ALAN: Yes, yes of course… semi-yon…

She goes into the kitchen. ALAN *crumples.*

SCARLETT: It's that guy again. He wants the chicken.
GARY: I don't want to cook it if he's going to do a runner again.
SCARLETT: No, I think he'll stay.

GARY *starts the chicken.*

GARY: What is with that guy?
SCARLETT: I wish I knew.
GORDON: Any sign of Shelley yet?
SCARLETT: No.
GORDON: She's never late.
GARY: I reckon she might be in a stew over Stu.
GORDON: [*to* GARY, *suspicious*] Did you phone Shelley's boyfriend?
GARY: Yep.
SCARLETT: You told him she was going out with Stu Dundell?
GARY: Yep.
GORDON: Keep taking the arsehole tablets, Gary—they're working.
GARY: Yeah, well she's just such a slut.
GORDON: Do you get them to keep their school uniforms on?
GARY: Shut up.
GORDON: How come you didn't say 'Shut up, you old poof'?
GARY: Sometimes I forget.
SCARLETT: Try and forget a bit more often.
GARY: What? Have you joined the freakin' thought police too?

SCARLETT *goes back to the banquette with* ALAN'*s semillon as* GORDON *re-enters.*

SCARLETT: Here's your semillon.
ALAN: Semillon. I really got that wrong, didn't I?

SCARLETT: Don't worry, tons of people get that wrong. Some even call cabernet, cabernet.

> ALAN *laughs.* SCARLETT *goes back into the restaurant.*

ALAN: [*practising the right pronunciation*] Cabernet…

GARY: Hey, those salt and peppers need doing. Freak'n Shelley.

> *In the kitchen* SCARLETT *backtracks to take* ALAN *his bread or condiments, but has a collision with the late arriving* SHELLEY. SHELLEY'*s nerves are at breaking point and she goes ballistic.*

SHELLEY: Scarlett!

SCARLETT: Sorry. Really sorry.

SHELLEY: Show me your right hand, Scarlett! Show it to me. Come on, show it!

> *She grabs the startled* SCARLETT'*s right hand and waves it in the air, spilling pepper on* SCARLETT'*s face.*

That's it, right? Do you think you can possibly remember? Then you'll be able to do 'in right, out right' and I won't forever be landing on my ass on the floor!

> *She breaks down and cries hysterically. They all realise that there's more to this than the collision.* SCARLETT *moves towards her.*

SCARLETT: Shelley, are you okay?

> SHELLEY *can't bring herself to tell them. She just shakes her head violently.* SCARLETT *puts her arm around her and spills salt and pepper on* SHELLEY.

What happened?

SHELLEY: I feel so degraded. So totally degraded. He took me to a lovely restaurant. He took me dancing. He took me home to his place… [*She sobs again.*] His teammates arrived. The complete midfield. He wanted me… to… with all of them. Said it would be terrific for team bonding. [*She howls.*] I just ran. Got straight into a cab and went straight to Derek and told him everything. He was so supportive. He didn't even seem surprised. I am so lucky to have him. So lucky.

> *She howls again.* STEVE *appears, and trips over salt and pepper shakers.*

STEVE: Jesus H Christ! What's been going on here?

SCARLETT: [*explaining to* STEVE] Shelley's had a midfield crisis.
SHELLEY: I've just learnt a very important lesson in life.
She sobs again.
STEVE: Well, good. Here's another. I just had the bank on the phone. If things don't turn round in the next few weeks they're going to close us down. [*Beat.*] I'm working on a totally new menu but if that doesn't work, it's finito.
STEVE moves out again towards his offstage office. There's a silence.
GARY: We should've had a new menu months ago. If this was my place, I'd...
SHELLEY: Well, it's not, so shut up.
GARY: I'd do tapas. Sweeping the world. The grazing instinct...
GORDON: Perfect for a bullshit artist like you.
GARY: Small portions, pervert. Small portions. You can order three, four, five. Chilli chicken torizo, maple mustard, lamb and merguez sausage skewers, chilli chicken torizo... I could go on.
SCARLETT: And on and on and on. Yes, we know.
GARY: But shit-for-brains in there won't listen so I'm considering my options...
GORDON: That would take all of three seconds.
GARY: For your information the buzz about me is getting louder.
GORDON: Yes, the blowflies do head straight for you.
GARY: Shut up, you old poof. [*To* SCARLETT] Take the gimp out his chicken.
GORDON: Well, before the rush starts I might pop out for a fag.
GORDON exits. SCARLETT takes the plate and goes out to ALAN. She sets the plate down in front of him. He smiles.
ALAN: Thank you.
As SCARLETT heads back to the kitchen, ALAN speaks nervously.
I've got another joke. Would you like to hear it?
SCARLETT: Ah, maybe not just now, Alan.
ALAN: [*crestfallen*] Oh, er, sure.
SCARLETT: Okay. Go on. Tell it.
She sits next to him.
ALAN: Thank you... But don't laugh just to make me feel better.

SCARLETT: Alan, I have to warn you that right at this moment there is no chance in hell I will laugh unless you're Laurel and 'ckin' Hardy.
ALAN: [*daunted but determined*] Right. This woman gets on a bus with a small baby and the bus driver looks at the baby and says, 'My God, that's the ugliest baby I've ever seen'. And the woman is so upset she's speechless and walks to the back of the bus and sits down next to this old lady. And then she turns to the old lady and says, 'That bus driver was very rude to me', so the old lady says, 'Well, you just go and tell that bus driver not to be so rude and, here, let me hold your monkey'.

> SCARLETT *really laughs.*

That was okay?
SCARLETT: Yes, very funny.

> *She gets up and pats him affectionately on the shoulder.*

ALAN: At least I didn't forget the punchline.
SCARLETT: Keep it in your repertoire. Enjoy your chicken.
ALAN: [*pleased with himself*] I will.

> ALAN *smiles at her. She smiles back and heads for the kitchen.*

Scarlett...

> SCARLETT *turns.*

[*With supreme effort*] Does your husband or... er... boyfriend, er... ever eat here?
SCARLETT: I haven't got a husband, Alan, and I haven't got a boyfriend.
ALAN: Really?
SCARLETT: Why so surprised?
ALAN: Well, you're... er... you're really... er... so... pretty.
SCARLETT: Thank you, Alan. That's the nicest thing that's been said to me for roughly... thirty-six years.

> ALAN *beams shyly and looks away.* SCARLETT *looks at him. There's something very disarming about him. Her film imagination is triggered again. Jimmy Stewart playing Mike and Katharine Hepburn playing Tracy in* The Philadelphia Story. *They start the scene up on the screen with Jimmy telling Katharine how much he admires her, then* ALAN *and* SCARLETT *take over. They kiss.*

ACT ONE

SCARLETT: Golly—

Another kiss.

Golly Moses!

ALAN: Let me tell you something, Scarlett…

SCARLETT: No, no—all of a sudden I've got the shakes.

ALAN: It can't be anything like love, can it?

SCARLETT: No, no, it mustn't be. It can't.

ALAN: Would it be inconvenient?

SCARLETT: Terribly.

STEVE enters from his office, excitement in his voice.

GARY: Hey, Rainwoman! Rinse the rosella flowers for the wattle seed pavlova. I'm gonna thaw the vindaloo.

STEVE: Scarlett!

SCARLETT hurries into the kitchen as STEVE comes bursting out of his office with the local newspaper still in his hand.

The environment thing you were talking about. It says here in the local paper that the postcode we're in here votes nearly fifty percent green.

SCARLETT: Really?

STEVE: [*nodding*] Could be what I've been looking for. No steak, no battery chicken and no press-ganged pigs. The world's first carbon neutral menu.

SCARLETT: Yeah? What would we serve?

STEVE: Cutting-edge vegetarian. There's an enviro dollar out there, Scarlett, and I want some.

He spontaneously embraces her and swings her around. He releases her. She's dumbstruck and stares at him. In her mind she is again transported to Gone with the Wind *as Rhett (*STEVE*) kisses Scarlett (herself).*

SCARLETT: Steve, don't, I shall faint.

STEVE: I want you to faint. This is what you were meant for. None of the fools you've ever known have kissed you like this, have they? Your Roger or your Frank or your stupid Alan.

The coolroom door slams. GARY*'s voice snaps her out of it.*

GARY: What's going on here?

STEVE: The lady molto grosso has not yet sung.

He goes back into his office. Up on the screen we see the breathless trailer for a forthcoming contemporary movie. Images of SCARLETT, ALAN *and* STEVE *appear on the screen as we have seen them during the first act.*

VOICE-OVER: 'She was in love with the chef.'

Shots of STEVE *and* SCARLETT.

'But was his heart still imprisoned by his elegant, beautiful, but faithless Parisian wife?'

Shots of STEVE*'s elegant, beautiful, faithless wife.*

Shots of SCARLETT *looking adoringly at* STEVE.

'Would her heart be crushed beyond repair? Or is the love she yearns for there, right under her nose?'

Shots of the nervous ALAN *staring wistfully at* SCARLETT.

'The scene is set for an extraordinarily poignant, achingly heartwarming, and totally predictable second act.'

On screen: 'Intermission' and the intermission music of Gone with the Wind *swells.*

END OF ACT ONE

ACT TWO

As the house lights go down, on the screen: 'You Ought To Be In Pictures' from Starlift.

SCENE ONE: NEW MENU, NEW DATE

STEVE *comes in excited with his new menus and hands them around to his staff who are all there doing prep.*

STEVE: New menu. Haven't slept for two days, but I think it's going to be good.

> *They look at it. He waits for reactions. They don't come. He starts to look nervous.* GARY *puts his menu down and recommences his preparation.*

Well?

SCARLETT: I think it's great, Steve.

STEVE: Gary?

GARY: It's your restaurant, mate. I'll do whatever you tell me to.

STEVE: Yeah, but what do you think?

GARY: Doesn't matter what I think, it's your restaurant.

STEVE: Gary, I want to know what you think.

GORDON: [*dubious*] A carbon equivalent for each dish?

SHELLEY: All vegetables grown with animal-sourced fertilizer? What's that mean?

GARY: Sprayed with pigshit. Do you seriously think people are going to say, 'This bean casserole only added fifty-five grams of carbon to the atmosphere, so I'll try it?'

SCARLETT: If we don't do something now, we're all going to be underwater in twenty years.

GARY: This menu is freakin' one hundred percent vegetarian.

STEVE: Cutting-edge, trail-blazing vegetarian.

GARY: Bloody hell! What's this? Pan-seared penne and chokos? Penne's the world's dullest pasta. And chokos?

STEVE: They're almost totally carbon neutral.
GARY: They're also flavour neutral, texture neutral and nourishment neutral.
STEVE: It's the sauce that counts. Read the sauce!
GARY: [*reading*] 'Naga Sabi sauce will leave behind a mushroom cloud of pain and leave you wanting more?'
GORDON: Could be a tad culturally insensitive, Steve.
STEVE: How's that?
GORDON: Japanese sauce, mushroom cloud.
STEVE: Fuck the Japanese! If we wanted Japanese, we'd serve whale meat!
SHELLEY: I can't see why there's all this fuss about things getting a little bit hotter. Personally I love summer.
SCARLETT: Good, because you'll shortly be getting it all year round.
SHELLEY: The world's always going to end according to the caffe latte set. I just get on with life.
SCARLETT: So we've noticed.
GARY: Mate, I've got to be honest. On the scale of good ideas, this one's somewhere between hiring Monica Lewinsky or leaving your wife with Wayne Carey. Change this menu or we're stuffed.
STEVE: [*banging his fist*] Like it our not, I've gone down this path and I'm expecting you all to try and make it work. I'm closing the restaurant tomorrow and Thursday while Gary and I get up to speed on the recipes. On Friday you three come in an hour early to brush up on the menu. And I expect a hundred percent commitment!

He looks around at them all.

SCARLETT: You've got it, Steve.
STEVE: I don't care what the odds are. I intend to fight!

> STEVE *heads out into the restaurant with the specials board.* SCARLETT *stands there transfixed by his glint-eyed determination, sparking a re-run of the Tarzan sequence from earlier.*
>
> *Lost in her world,* SCARLETT *leaps onto the laundry basket, bellowing the iconic Tarzan call. The fantasy abruptly ends with the others all staring at her.*

SCARLETT: [*embarrassed*] Johnny Weissmuller. *Tarzan and His Mate.* 1934.

ACT TWO

GARY shakes his head and goes out to the coolroom, muttering in Greek.

SHELLEY: Poor Steve. I shouldn't tell you this, and keep it quiet, but his wife's gone back to France.

SCARLETT: He told you?

SHELLEY: I was walking past his office last Saturday and he had tears in his eyes. He wasn't going to tell me, but then he said I was the one person he felt he could trust.

SCARLETT looks crestfallen. STEVE comes back from the restaurant.

STEVE: Grange Hermitage is back. He's waiting in the banquette.

SHELLEY: [*to* SCARLETT] My turn.

SCARLETT: He's not rich. The Grange Hermitage was a mistake.

SHELLEY: He's all yours.

SCARLETT: [*defiantly*] I quite like him.

SHELLEY: [*condescending*] I suppose you have left your run a little late for Mr Perfect.

SCARLETT: Shelley, he's nice. That's it. I don't lie awake quivering at the thought of his hot breath on my nipples.

SHELLEY: Hot breath? That guy couldn't warm a pie.

She walks out into the restaurant and moves disdainfully past ALAN even though he's much more sharply dressed than last time.

The other waitress will attend to you.

SCARLETT, who has followed SHELLEY out, smiles at ALAN.

SCARLETT: Back again?

ALAN: Yeah, I hope that's okay.

SCARLETT: We're glad to have you. I'll just get you some water.

ALAN: No, no. It's fine.

She starts to hand him the menu, but he doesn't want it.

The chicken.

SCARLETT: You're sure you wouldn't like to see the menu?

ALAN: No, the chicken.

SCARLETT: The whole menu's changing. Last chance for the kangaroo.

ALAN: No…

SCARLETT: Or the buffalo. It's still on the menu.

ALAN: No, the chicken. [*Attempting to be a man of the world*] If you like something, no sense changing.

SCARLETT: You could be right, Alan, but on the other hand sometimes something new can come into your life and it can be magic. When I was little the only film I'd seen was *Gone with the Wind*. Mum never missed a screening of it. Then one day when I was seven I was sent to stay with my Great Aunt Violet while Mum had a new carpet laid. Aunty Violet lived with my other Aunt Clara who wasn't really my aunt, they a shared a bed which I found a bit strange, but Aunt Violet said it was to save on washing powder. Anyway, the weekend they took me along to this little old art deco cinema and for the first time I saw *The Wizard of Oz* and *Calamity Jane* and *Snow White and the Seven Dwarfs*. We saw *Queen Christina* quite a few times, but the point is a whole new world opened up, a world of romance and danger and excitement—but sorry, I'm carrying on again.

ALAN: No, no. You've got a point. Is there, er, something else good—except the kangaroo and buffalo?

SCARLETT: Actually chicken is probably the next best.

ALAN: [*relieved*] Great. The chicken.

SCARLETT: And a glass of the Grange?

ALAN: Ah.

> *She smiles and starts to move off.*

Ah... Scarlett...

SCARLETT: Mmm.

ALAN: [*very difficult for him*] Do you ever get a night off?

SCARLETT: Usually Monday, but this week we've got two nights while Steve prepares the new menu.

ALAN: [*excited*] Starting tomorrow?

SCARLETT: And Thursday.

ALAN: Ah, there's this very good concert on tomorrow night. I er... don't suppose er... that there's a possibility that you might... er, like to come?

> *He's not exactly* SCARLETT*'s dream date. How can she get out of it?*

SCARLETT: Alan, that's so nice of you but I've gone off concerts ever since a friend of my cousin's friend got crushed in a mosh pit and was on a respirator for four days.

ALAN: No, no. Not heavy metal. It's the Melbourne Symphony Orchestra, playing the great film scores.

SCARLETT: The great film scores?

ALAN: [*handing her the flyer*] *Gone with the Wind, Calamity Jane, Oklahoma*—it's under the stars at the zoo.

She's tempted, but no, he isn't her preferred date. SCARLETT*'s imagination again wanders to* Gone with the Wind. *In her mind,* STEVE *becomes Rhett.*

STEVE: It's not that easy, Scarlett. You turn me out, while you chase Alan, while you dream of Alan. This is one night you're not turning me out.

They ascend the stairs

SCARLETT: [*thinking hard, lying*] Ah, the zoo. What a pity. I have a real allergy problem with imported animals. They think it might be the llamas or the meerkats.

ALAN: They make a special seating area. At the other end from the meerkats.

He can see her hesitation.

Look, I know I probably come across as a little bit…

SCARLETT: [*embarrassed*] No, no.

ALAN: I've been listening to those old film soundtracks and they're great. [*He sings and isn't too bad.*] 'When I'm calling you-oo-oo-oo-oo-oo-oo…'

SCARLETT *stops, turns.*

SCARLETT: 'Will you answer true-oo-oo-oo-oo-oo-oo…'

SHELLEY *sweeps past looking disdainful.* SCARLETT *takes exception to her disdain. She looks at* ALAN.

Alright, Alan. That would be nice.

And suddenly Jeanette MacDonald and Nelson Eddy are up on the big screen oo-ing 'Indian Love Call' from Rose-Marie. SCARLETT *joins them.*

SCENE TWO: THE GREEN PARROT

Friday, 5.32 p.m. STEVE *and* GARY *are hard at work on the prep.* GARY *starts singing to the tune of Abba's 'Money, Money, Money'.*

GARY: 'Chokos, chokos chokos, Always chokos, It's a choko world.'
STEVE: Gary.
GARY: No, I'm coming to love 'em, boss. They remind me of nipples.
STEVE: Is there anything in the world that doesn't remind you of some part of the female anatomy?
GARY: [*thinking, then admitting*] It is hard.
STEVE: I'm going to write up the specials. Just be on your toes. This is a big night. No stuff-ups.
GARY: I'm in the zone, boss. I just stare at my hands and can't believe what they're doing.

    SHELLEY *arrives as he says it.*

SHELLEY: Could be a good defence when you're up on your next sex charge.
GARY: So which team was it last night? Collingwood?
SHELLEY: You think it's a joke. I'm still freaked by it. Will be for years.
GARY: What are you? Naive? Guys like Stu Dundell can have any woman they want. Why do you think they chose you?
SHELLEY: You are rock bottom, snake's ass, worm's whanger, low.
GARY: I'm not saying you're not a horny chick. You bloody are. I'm trying to level with you so you don't get hurt again.
SHELLEY: Oh, you've got a deep concern.
GARY: That guy Derek Targus's never going to marry you. Get real.
SHELLEY: For your information, he's shopping for a ring right now.

    SCARLETT *comes in.*

SCARLETT: This is exciting. The 'Green Parrot'.
GARY: The Green Parrot?
SCARLETT: Didn't you read the new sign?
GARY: The Green freakin' Parrot?
SCARLETT: Worked out well. The walls were green already.

    GORDON *enters with the local paper.*

GORDON: Oh, my dears! Steve's put a huge ad in the local paper. 'Respect the planet. Eat carbon neutral.' Stand back and wait for the stampede.

ACT TWO

STEVE comes back from the office with the specials board.

STEVE: Move it, guys. They'll be coming through the doors any minute. Gordon, take this out to the restaurant.

GORDON: Fricassee of fava beans. My favourite!

As GORDON leaves, STEVE throws himself into the prep with great energy.

STEVE: Gary! Shelley, marinate the tofu. Where're the leeks?

GARY: [*pointing to the ceiling*] There's one there and one there. Why, is it going to rain?

STEVE: Gary, Jerry Seinfeld is very rich and you're chopping chokos, why do you think that is? Where are the fucking leeks?

GARY: In the coolroom. Along with three hundred and twenty other varieties of vegetable.

STEVE storms out grumpily. GORDON returns from the restaurant.

GORDON: [*to* SCARLETT] What was the concert like?

SCARLETT: Amazing. All the great movie tunes. Elephants made a bit of a noise, but that seemed to add to it.

GARY: Was our sprinter hot in the cot?

SCARLETT: Gary! I went to a concert. Full stop.

GORDON: Not even a kiss? A peck on the cheek?

SCARLETT: So who have we here? Yente the village matchmaker?

STEVE comes out of the coolroom with an arm full of leeks.

GARY: [*to* STEVE] Scarlett's rooting the bolter.

STEVE: What?

SCARLETT: [*embarrassed*] I went to a concert. I felt sorry for him.

SHELLEY: [*condescendingly*] I think it's great that Scarlett's found someone at last.

SCARLETT: He had a spare ticket!

SHELLEY: I think he's quite cute in a totally dorky way.

SCARLETT: He's not my type at all.

GARY: Who is your type?

SCARLETT: [*trying not to look at* STEVE] Older man. Mature. Someone with the courage to keep fighting when things are going bad. How are the bookings, Steve?

STEVE: Should be great. Gordon, check the book. I put a really big ad in the local paper, looked fantastic. [*Beat.*] Well.

GORDON *looks in the book.*

GORDON: One.

STEVE: One. We've got one booking?

GORDON: Table for one. Gore. Six-thirty.

STEVE: [*staring at the book*] It was a really prominent ad. Phone message bank must be out of order. I'll check. Gordon, finish the leeks.

SCARLETT: [*calling after him*] Don't worry, Steve. We'll make this work by word of mouth.

GORDON: Let's hope Mr Gore's got a very big mouth.

> SHELLEY *looks out into the restaurant to see if anyone's arrived.* ALAN *is sitting in the banquette.*

SHELLEY: Make that two bookings. [*To* SCARLETT] Your boyfriend's back.

SCARLETT: Alan?

> *She picks up a menu and hurries out.* SHELLEY *beats her to it, eager to quiz* ALAN.

SHELLEY: Alan? Scarlett said the concert was wonderful.

ALAN: Oh. Really?

SHELLEY: Loved it. Absolutely loved it.

> SCARLETT *appears, grim faced.*

ALAN: [*nervously looking at* SCARLETT] Really?

SHELLEY: The stars, the moon, the romantic tunes. Can't stop her talking about it. Can we, Scarlett?

SCARLETT: Thanks, Shelley.

SHELLEY: [*to* ALAN] Her hair's really nice tonight, don't you think?

SCARLETT: *Thanks, Shelley!*

> SHELLEY *beams at them and goes back to the kitchen.*

ALAN: You did like the concert?

SCARLETT: Yes, I did. Very much.

ALAN: No problem from the meerkats?

SCARLETT: The meerkats? Oh, the meerkats. Not a sniffle.

ALAN: I thought it was magic. I never knew those old tunes would be so…

SCARLETT: So what?

ALAN: Romantic. What about that one at the end—what's that from? [*He sings.*] 'If I loved you, Time and again I would try to say…'

Caroline O'Connor as Scarlett and Matt Day as Alan, in the 2008 MTC production. (Photo: Jeff Busby)

SCARLETT: *Carousel.* Shirley Jones and Gordon MacRae. 1957. [*She sings.*] 'If I loved you, Words wouldn't come in an easy way...'
SCARLETT & ALAN: [*singing, together*] 'Round in circles I'd go...'

> *And suddenly in* SCARLETT's *imagination we're up on the big screen again in the famous scene between Elizabeth Taylor and Montgomery Clift in* A Place in the Sun. SCARLETT *plays Liz and she casts* ALAN *as Monty.*

SCARLETT: I love you too. And it scares me. But it is a wonderful feeling.
ALAN: Oh, Scarlett, if only I could only tell you how much I love you. If I could only tell you all.
SCARLETT: Tell Scarlett. Tell Scarlett all.

> SCARLETT's *split loyalties cause her to snap out of the fantasy, confused.*

Ah. The menu?

> ALAN *looks at the menu.*

ALAN: Thank you. [*A little alarmed*] This has changed.
SCARLETT: Yes, very exciting.
ALAN: But I loved the chicken.
SCARLETT: Alan, you wouldn't want to get stuck in a rut.

> *This strikes a warning note for* ALAN.

ALAN: No, mustn't get in a rut. [*Looking again at the menu*] That hot one. The mushroom cloud? Is it very hot?
SCARLETT: I'd say so.
ALAN: You haven't tried it?
SCARLETT: No.
ALAN: Ah, well, what the hell. [*He frowns. Second thoughts*] Ah, is it very, very hot?
SCARLETT: Would you like to change to something else?

> *He glances at the menu, then suddenly gets resolute.*

ALAN: No, let's stick with it. What kind of life is it if you never walk on the wild side?

> SCARLETT *tries to keep a smile off her face. This guy is seriously weird but in an endearing sort of way.*

SCARLETT: One mushroom cloud coming up.

> *On screen, Atlanta in flames from* Gone with the Wind.

ACT TWO

SCENE THREE: AFTERMATH

Next day, 6.10 p.m. STEVE, SHELLEY *and* GARY *are in the kitchen.* SCARLETT *arrives.*

GORDON: How is he?

SCARLETT: Just out of intensive care. The mushroom cloud sent him into anaphylactic shock. They had to force an oxygen tube down his throat to keep him breathing.

STEVE: Is he going to sue?

SCARLETT: Thanks for your concern, Steve. No, I don't think so. In fact he said the funniest thing. Well, actually he couldn't say it. Tubes down his throat. [*She acts out how hard it was for him to talk.*] He wrote it down.

She shows them what ALAN *wrote.*

STEVE: [*reading*] 'That would have to be the most unforgettable meal I ever had.' No, that doesn't sound like someone who's going to sue. [*Without thinking he puts the note on the shelf.*] Thank God for small mercies. Scarlett, help Shelley with the desserts.

SCARLETT *hurries to help* SHELLEY.

Gordon, how many bookings?

GORDON: [*to* STEVE] Seven.

STEVE: Seven! We're a shipwreck and there ain't no lifeboats. You all better take any other jobs that are on offer.

GARY: I'm fine.

STEVE: You've got a job?

GARY: Sous chef at Jacques Reymond.

GORDON: Jacques Reymond?

STEVE: Are you kidding me?

GARY: I'm first on the short list.

STEVE: Have they been taken over by Hungry Jacks?

GARY: [*shrugging nonchalantly*] Typical Baby Boomer. Fresh new talent under your nose and you just didn't notice.

STEVE: No, no, Gary. I did. That night when you attempted coq au vin and it actually tasted like chicken, I went out the back and cried. Shelley, you'll be okay, won't you? That guy you're marrying is loaded.

SHELLEY *bursts into tears.*

GORDON: What's wrong?

GARY: He gave her the flick, like I always knew he would.

SHELLEY: It wasn't Derek. It was his mother. Okay, my lawyer dug his heels in over the pre-nup, but to call me Australia's Heather Mills was outrageous.

GORDON: It certainly was.

GARY: You've got twice as many legs.

> SCARLETT *comes across to comfort her. Problem is* SHELLEY's *still got the cream squeezing gadget in her hand and as* SCARLETT *hugs her she manages to squirt raspberry coulis all down* SHELLEY's *blouse.* SHELLEY *shrieks.*

SCARLETT: That's it, Shell, let it out.

SHELLEY: Scarlett!

> *She turns and offloads more coulis onto* STEVE.
>
> SCARLETT *moves towards* GARY *with the cream gadget.*

GARY: Scarlett. [*As if he's talking to someone with a gun*] Put down the raspberry coulis. Slowly. Slowly. Good girl.

> SHELLEY *runs towards the washroom.* GARY *goes to the coolroom.* GORDON *takes rubbish outside.* STEVE *starts gloomily wiping raspberry off himself.* SCARLETT *moves to him.*

SCARLETT: I'm so sorry, Steve. I think the new menu's terrific. Everyone who comes says the food is much, much better than they expected.

STEVE: Frankly, it's the best menu I've ever done. Impose limitations and you have to be doubly creative to work within 'em, but unless I can think of a way to get enough people in here to start word of mouth, it really is all over.

> SCARLETT *nods glumly.* STEVE *snaps out of it.*

SCARLETT: Oh, Steve. Don't worry about anything. You needn't worry.

> *On the screen she becomes her exhausted namesake from* Gone with the Wind. *The others also take up roles:* GORDON *becomes Mammy,* SHELLEY *becomes Piccaninny and* GARY *a servant.*

GORDON: Miss Scarlett, what are we going to do with nothing to feed those sick folks and that child?

SCARLETT: I don't know, Mammy. I don't know.

GORDON: We ain't got nothin' but radishes in the garden.
SHELLEY: Miss Scarlett, I don't know nothin' about soakin' mung beans. I only got two hands.
GARY: I told you all along, Miss Scarlett, we should have done tapas.

> SCARLETT *wanders outside to survey the sun setting on the arid fields.*

SCENE FOUR: LATE NIGHT FANTASIES

Later that night. GARY *is alone reading a newspaper in the banquette.* SCARLETT *passes with her arms full of tablecloths.*

SCARLETT: Why are you still here?
GARY: Someone's picking me up. A woman I met.
SCARLETT: That sounds promising.
GARY: What does?
SCARLETT: She must be old enough to have a driver's licence.
GARY: Yeah, good joke, good joke. The truth is she was a total exception. Most of the women I root are married chicks in their thirties like this one tonight.
SCARLETT: So where did you meet her?
GARY: On the 109 Tram to Box Hill. I see this gorgeous woman looking at me. So I smile back. She's getting off the tram, and suddenly there's this bit of paper in my hand. Her phone number. Look, I'm not boasting, Scarls, but I never have to try too hard. In fact my problem is it's all too easy.
SCARLETT: So what happens when she gets here?
GARY: She's booked a suite at the Sofitel, a bit of champagne, *Gladiators*, and five times, six times. She's happy, I'm happy. Look, I don't want to blow my own trumpet, Scarls, but the sad truth is most husbands are hopeless in the cot. Time after time these women say to me, 'Gary, I never had any idea it could be like this'.
SCARLETT: Be like what?
GARY: Basically women don't want wimps. They want someone who takes command. They've got to feel the confidence, feel the heat. They've got to look in your eyes and know you're going to take them where they've never been.

> SCARLETT *is finding herself sucked in and excited, despite herself.*

You've got to strut your stuff. What's that word in those old movies of yours where the hero gets out his sword and fights all the bad guys?

SCARLETT: Swashbuckling.

GARY: That's it. You've got to be swashbuckling. That's what they want. Swashbuckling.

> *This triggers* SCARLETT'*s film imagination again. Up on the large screen, Errol Flynn, as Robin Hood, fights his way out of the Sheriff of Nottingham's castle. No matter that he's outnumbered a thousand to one, he dispatches his enemy with superb swordplay, exuding arrogant confidence.*
>
> SCARLETT'*s mind leaps to the scene in which Robin (*GARY*) asks Maid Marian (*SCARLETT*) to come to Sherwood.*

GARY: Marian, will you come with me?

SCARLETT: To Sherwood?

GARY: I've nothing to offer you but a life of hardship and danger, but we'd be together.

> *They kiss. The kiss becomes quite torrid. Robin starts to rip Marian's clothes off.*
>
> SCARLETT *snaps out of it and leaps back in horror at the thought of kissing* GARY. *She shudders.*

GARY: Are you okay?

SCARLETT: [*blushing*] Yes. Yes.

> *A taxi toots.* GARY *throws on his coat.*

GARY: Gotta go. Honey babe, here comes the pleasure machine.

> *He races out.* SCARLETT *takes a half-empty bottle of white wine and gulps it down. She goes into the kitchen. She puts the tablecloths into the basket, pausing for a moment to fantasise that they're a man. She shakes off the fantasy and has another drink.* STEVE *comes in.*

STEVE: Scarlett? Are you okay?

SCARLETT: Yeah. Just resting.

STEVE: I didn't think you drank?

SCARLETT: I've started.

STEVE: Give me some too.

He slumps down beside her. She tries to cheer him up.

SCARLETT: Fourteen covers tonight. Creeping up.

STEVE: Creeping's the word. I saw the bank manager. End of next week. Sending in the auditors.

SCARLETT: Have you tried to get any critics in?

STEVE: They won't come. Ironically, the only ringing endorsement we've had in print is your friend Alan's note.

Reading Alan's note again, STEVE *then puts it back on the shelf.*

SCARLETT: The most unforgettable meal he's ever had.

She pours him some wine. He gulps it down. She does the same. He shakes his head.

Ah, don't worry, she'll come back.

STEVE: I don't want her back.

SCARLETT: Really? Never?

STEVE: Never. Marry a beautiful woman and your life is agony. For their whole life, people have gasped, doors have opened, men have flocked around. They've got this huge sense of entitlement. They think luxury is their birthright.

SCARLETT: Really?

STEVE: And you've got to have eyes in the back of your head to see who's chatting them up next.

SCARLETT: I hadn't thought of that.

STEVE: Yeah, marry someone beautiful and you pay a price. It wasn't until she went I realised how miserable she made me. Not that I'd want to marry a dog, but if I had my time over again I'd go for the middle range.

SCARLETT: [*preening herself*] For example?

STEVE *looks straight into her eyes and holds the gaze.*

STEVE: Someone like Shelley.

SCARLETT *tries not to look crushed.*

Not that I'd ever contemplate her. Even though she isn't, she thinks she's beautiful, so it would be high maintenance all over again.

SCARLETT: I'd better go.

STEVE: Scarlett.

SCARLETT: Yes.

STEVE: You mightn't be a world's best practice waitress, but you know something?

> *She shakes her head breathlessly. They look into each other's eyes.* SCARLETT*'s heart is beating fast.*

I like having you around.

SCARLETT: Really?

STEVE: [*nodding*] You accept your limitations and battle on.

> *It's not exactly a ringing endorsement, but it's enough for* SCARLETT *to send her film imagination into overdrive. She becomes Ingrid Bergman as Ilsa in* Casablanca.

INGRID/SCARLETT: I love you so much, and I hate this war so much. Oh, it's a crazy world. Anything can happen. If you shouldn't get away, I mean, if, if something should keep us apart, wherever they put you and wherever I'll be, I want you to know…

> *She can't go on. She lifts her face to his. He kisses her gently.*

Kiss me. Kiss me as if it were the last time.

> SCARLETT *tries to snap out of the fantasy as usual, but something is wrong. This is no fantasy. She is kissing* STEVE. *She draws back in horror.*

SCARLETT: I didn't mean that to happen, really. [*Blurting it out*] But I'm not sorry.

STEVE: Scarlett, it's late at night and we've been drinking. I'm sure you'll understand that I've got to be very sure of my headspace before I even begin to contemplate any new relationship.

SCARLETT: Of course. I'm sorry. I'm so embarrassed.

STEVE: No, no. You're a very special person, it's just that—

SCARLETT: [*moving to get her bike helmet*] I know, headspace, Madeleine, daughters, dog—

STEVE: But don't think that I was just taking— [*advantage*]

SCARLETT: No, I don't, I don't, I really don't, but—yeah

> *She goes.* STEVE *remains sitting there. We think that maybe he's contemplating the encounter with* SCARLETT, *but no, that's all but forgotten. His eyes fall again on the note that* ALAN *wrote* SCARLETT. *He picks it up and reads it again, snorting ironically, then suddenly it triggers something in his memory. He gets up,*

newly energised, and races across to the book in which the bookings are written. He thumbs back through it with growing excitement. He finds what he's looking for and lets out a whoop of delight.

STEVE: Yahoo!

Cut to film footage of a Robin Hood feast scene.

ROBIN: May I serve you, my lady?
MARIAN: I'm afraid your company has spoiled my appetite.
ROBIN: Ah, misfortune. Not mine, it's excellent.

SCENE FIVE: ALAN RETURNS, GARY LEAVES

One week later, 8.52 p.m. The kitchen is busy. SCARLETT *enters from the restaurant, carrying dirty plates.*

GARY: Table Seven, good to go. One smoked alfalfa roulade, one chive and chickpea enchilada and a parsnip in a pear coulis.
SCARLETT: It's amazing. We're totally full again tonight.
STEVE: And most of the rest of next week. I'm having a little party to celebrate at the end of the night.
GARY: Sorry, mate. Got a little action lined up after work, if you know what I mean.
GORDON: Yes, she called. She wants you to wait around the block in case the headmistress sees her climbing out the dormitory window.
GARY: She's got a younger brother if you're interested.
SCARLETT: [*to* STEVE] I'd love to stay back for a little while.

> SCARLETT *picks up two plates and heads out into the restaurant, as* SHELLEY *comes in from the restaurant.*

SHELLEY: Stay back for what?
GORDON: Party time.
SHELLEY: Boy, could I use it after last night.
GARY: What happened last night?
SHELLEY: Don't ask me.
GARY: Okay.
GORDON: [*filling in the silence*] The blind date?
SHELLEY: I wish I had've been blind. This guy was Michael Moore's ugly brother.

GARY: [*stroking his crotch suggestively*] Why waste your time, honey, when you've got three hundred grams of steak here any time you want it.

GORDON: Handfed.

> *Out in the restaurant* SCARLETT *stares.* ALAN *is back in his usual banquette. But he's looking the worse for wear. He still has cotton wool stuffed in his mouth.*

SCARLETT: Alan? You're back here?

ALAN: Wasn't your fault.

SCARLETT: Are you alright?

ALAN: Ah, yeah. All the lining of my mouth is still, er, scorched. Have to drink fluids through a straw still.

SCARLETT: We've, er, got a lentil broth.

ALAN: Ah, no, that's fine. I've already had my… er… the hospital sent me home with a week's Optifast. Pretty full tonight?

SCARLETT: Yeah, it's amazing. Apparently Steve's launched a whole new advertising campaign in the local paper. I haven't seen it yet but whatever it is, it seems to be working. So, er, you're not eating?

ALAN: Ah, no. I'm not staying.

SCARLETT: Oh.

ALAN: I just came to ask… I thought maybe… The concert was so much fun, maybe we could watch one of the movies…?

SCARLETT: That sounds nice.

ALAN: At your place.

SCARLETT: At my place?

ALAN: If that's alright?

SCARLETT: Well…

ALAN: *Casablanca*, maybe? 'Play it, Sam. Play "As Time goes By".'

> Casablanca *footage featuring* STEVE *as Humphrey Bogart.*

HUMPHREY/STEVE: Tell me, who was it you left me for? Was it Alan, or were there others in between? Or aren't you the kind to tell?

SCARLETT: Maybe in a week or two when things have settled down here?

ALAN: [*glumly*] Yeah. Sure.

> ALAN *slumps into the banquette as* SCARLETT *moves towards the kitchen. She turns and sees him as Jimmy Stewart in* It's a Wonderful Life.

ALAN: Help me, Scarlett. Help me please.
SCARLETT: No really, I'd be happy to go out in a week or two.
ALAN: Really?

> *She nods. He leaves happily*
>
> *Meanwhile in the kitchen,* GARY's *mobile phone rings. He answers. He listens. His smile grows broader.*

GARY: [*almost shrieking*] You're kidding! You're kidding! [*He switches off the phone and shrieks with triumph.*] I got the gig!
GORDON: Jacques Reymond?
GARY: Television chef! They said my screen test had the producers drooling. They said I've got more screen charisma than Jamie Oliver. Leapt off the screen.
SHELLEY: You're going on television?
GARY: For sure, mate, for freakin' sure. They're after a younger audience.
STEVE: Your chocolate muffins will absolutely lock in the under-sevens.
GARY: Mate, it's a different world. Charisma, youth—you just don't get it, do you?
SHELLEY: What channel, Gary?
GARY: Cable. That's where the cutting edge is these days. [*He takes off his apron as he whoops again.*] So long, suckers!
STEVE: You're walking out? Right now.
GARY: Bloody oath.
SCARLETT: Whatever happened to loyalty?
GARY: Loyalty, mate? [*He laughs.*] I'm Generation Y. [*To* STEVE] Put the money you owe me in the mail, Steve. [*He goes, stopping as he walks out through the restaurant. To the diners*] Don't bother staying. The food will be shit. Elvis has just left the building.

> *Film clip: Shane retreats into the distance in* Shane.

SCENE SIX: PARTY

That night. The celebration has been underway some time. As happens in most parties, the participants have split up. Out in the restaurant, SCARLETT *is talking to* GORDON *in the banquette, while* SHELLEY *is talking to* STEVE *in the kitchen. The dialogue is intercut and somewhat overlapping. Everyone's more than a little drunk.*

The kitchen:

SHELLEY: I just think it's terrible that he walked out just like that. A full restaurant.
STEVE: Total arsehole, always was.
SHELLEY: I thought you coped magnificently. Will you be able to get a replacement?
STEVE: Not for a week or two. But I'll cope.
SHELLEY: I'll give you all the help I can.

They look at each other.

The banquette:

SCARLETT: Gordon, I need to tell you something.
GORDON: 'Speak to me, Harry Winston, tell me all about it.'
SCARLETT: You won't tell anyone?
GORDON: Me? An aging old queen indulge in gossip?
SCARLETT: No, really.
GORDON: For you, my lips, while unable to stop pouting, are sealed.
SCARLETT: I've got a... really, really strong thing for...
GORDON: Who?
SCARLETT: Steve.
GORDON: [*shaking his head*] No.
SCARLETT: He kissed me, or rather I kissed him—but he responded.
GORDON: He's married.
SCARLETT: His wife's left him, taken the kids.
GORDON: No.
SCARLETT: I can't help it, Gordon. I can't get him out of my head. It's getting worse.

GORDON *says nothing.*

The kitchen:

SHELLEY: It's funny, Steve, when you work closely with someone the Americans have got a term for it. They call it a work husband or a work wife.
STEVE: Yeah, it gets like that, doesn't it?
SHELLEY: Nothing... sexual of course—
STEVE: Of course.

The banquette:

SCARLETT: I'm sick of putting myself down. I'm an attractive person in the prime of my life. Why wouldn't he be interested?

GORDON: Just be careful. In the scale of human misery a broken heart comes second only to irritable bowel syndrome.

SCARLETT: Careful? That's what I've been all my life. Careful? Why? Because I'm too gutless to take a risk. High board at the swimming pool? No, no. Little mouse Scarlett goes tippy-toe to the low board, and even that's too high. Jump in from the side at least? No! Slide in, carefully and slow. That's what I've been doing all my life. Sliding in carefully and slow. And where has it got me? The most boring life since Elizabeth Taylor fell in love with a pony in *National Velvet*. No more Little Miss Careful.

The kitchen:

SHELLEY *puts her hand on* STEVE'S *arm.*

SHELLEY: It's so awful about your wife.

They stare into each other's eyes. Suddenly they're embracing, passionately.

The banquette:

SCARLETT *gets up, her eyes blazing.*

SCARLETT: Fasten your seatbelt, Gordon. It's going to be a bumpy night!

She marches off to the kitchen.

GORDON: Bette Davis. *All About Steve*. 1950.

The kitchen:

Things have progressed very rapidly in the kitchen. When SCARLETT *sweeps through the door, she's greeted with the sight of* SHELLEY *on the bench with her legs in the air and* STEVE *fumbling with his fly. She stands stock still in shock, then as* SHELLEY *notices her, backs out of the door.*

Film footage: Mildred Pierce. SCARLETT *plays Mildred,* STEVE *Mildred's husband and* SHELLEY *takes on the role of Alveta.*

SCARLETT: Shelley.

STEVE: We weren't expecting you, Scarlett, obviously.

SHELLEY: It's just as well you know. I'm glad you know. He never loved you. It's always been me. And there's nothing you can do about it.

SCENE SEVEN: SCARLETT DRUNK

Later that night, 1.49 a.m. SCARLETT *stumbles into her flat. She doesn't turn on the light, so of course she crashes over everything it's possible to crash over as she heads for her bedroom. The noise brings her mother out in her dressing-gown with a baseball bat. She switches on the light. Both scream.* MAUREEN *hits the couch with the bat.*

MAUREEN: Oh, it's you! Have you been drinking?
SCARLETT: No. There's something I want to ask you.
MAUREEN: Not while you're drunk.
SCARLETT: I can only say it while I'm drunk. Sit down. I'll get you tea.
MAUREEN: I don't want tea.

>SCARLETT *is already staggering off but seems to have forgotten where the electric kettle is.*

SCARLETT: I'll get you tea.
MAUREEN: I don't want tea.
SCARLETT: Sit down! I'll get you tea. [*She doesn't.*] My life's going to shit and it's time to be honest.
MAUREEN: I wish you wouldn't say that word.
SCARLETT: Honest? Yeah, it's a very dangerous word.
MAUREEN: The 'S' word. I didn't bring you up to be vulgar.
SCARLETT: What did you bring me up to be, Mommy Dearest?
MAUREEN: Someone I'd be proud of.
SCARLETT: And I'm not. And sometimes that makes me very angry at myself and… you.
MAUREEN: Me?
SCARLETT: Yes you.
MAUREEN: It's normal for daughters to get a little angry with their mothers sometimes.
SCARLETT: Not a little. Really, really angry.
MAUREEN: I think you should go to bed.
SCARLETT: I have these terrible dreams.
MAUREEN: What sort of dreams?
SCARLETT: Knife-in-my-hand sort of dreams.
MAUREEN: Scarlett, I fought for you, they wanted me to have you—
SCARLETT: Yes I know. I could have been just a bloody foetus. All my life I've lived with the thought that the other me, the parallel

universe me, is a bloody foetus. I'm grateful, I'm grateful, but I just yearn…

MAUREEN: For what?

SCARLETT: … for the day when I do something, and you stare at me, and say, 'That was wonderful, Scarlett, I am really, really proud'.

MAUREEN: I'm sure I've done that often.

SCARLETT: Never! Not once!

MAUREEN: I'm sure.

SCARLETT: [*with a surge of passion*] Occasionally I would have liked to have felt—

MAUREEN: What?

SCARLETT: —that on balance, all things considered, taking the long view, and not to overstate it, you're actually glad I *happened*!

MAUREEN: [*amazed*] Darling, isn't it obvious? You're the best thing that ever happened in my life.

SCARLETT: You mean that? You really mean that?

> SCARLETT *runs across and hugs her mother passionately, over-passionately.* MAUREEN, *uncomfortable, wriggles to disengage herself.*

MAUREEN: My bones, Scarlett. My bones!

SCARLETT: The best thing that ever happened in your life?

MAUREEN: Of course! Mind you, frankly there's been very precious little competition.

> SCARLETT *disengages herself.*

Now, for God's sake, go to bed, and don't ever drink as much as you have tonight, again!

> *She grumps off to bed.* SCARLETT *sits there. A movie scene begins on screen. It's from* The Wizard of Oz.

DOROTHY: Some place where there isn't any trouble. Do you suppose there is such a place, Toto? There must be. It's not a place you can get to by a boat or a train. It's far, far away—behind the moon—beyond the rain—

> *On the screen, the young Judy Garland morphs into* SCARLETT.

SCARLETT: [*singing*] Somewhere, over the rainbow, way up high,
> There's a land that I heard of once in a lullaby.
> Somewhere, over the rainbow, skies are blue,

And the dreams that you dare to dream
Really do come true…

SCENE EIGHT: AL GORE

Next night, 5.43 p.m. The kitchen is frantic as STEVE, *now the lone chef, preps for the diners who will soon start arriving.* SHELLEY *is filling in for* GARY *and chopping vegetables.* GORDON *is frantically bringing in food from the coolroom.*

STEVE: Shelley! I asked you to *slice* the zucchini, not murder it.
SHELLEY: Steve, I'm a waitress.
STEVE: [*moving across to her angrily and taking the knife*] Like this, for fuck's sake! [*He does rapid chopping. Too rapid. He cuts his finger and swears.*] Fuckin' hell. Gordon!

> GORDON *knows the routine. He's got a bad hangover but manages to get across to the first-aid drawer and grab a band-aid.*

GORDON: Nurse Ratchet to the rescue. [*Holding his head*] And when I say rat shit I mean it.
STEVE: [*to* GORDON] Quick! It's not a good look to have blood in the ratatouille!
GORDON: I feel like I flew over the cuckoo nest last night.

> GORDON *winces at the volume of blood. He puts on the band-aid.*

STEVE: [*to* SHELLEY] Where the fuck is Scarlett? We're a chef down with a full fucking house due to arrive. Gordon, peel the chickpeas. Make a fucking effort, Shelley!
SHELLEY: Last night Casanova, tonight Gordon Ramsey!
STEVE: Don't mention last night. I should've known better.
GORDON: You seemed to know more than enough.

> SHELLEY, *eyes blazing, is about to take a knife to* GORDON. SCARLETT *comes in.*

STEVE: [*sarcastically*] Well, look who's here. Only forty-five minutes late.
SCARLETT: [*sarcastic back*] I thought you two might like some quality time together.
STEVE: [*exiting to the coolroom*] Scarlett, just help Shelley with the ratatouille.

ACT TWO 71

GORDON: [*to* SCARLETT, *indicating* SHELLEY] And don't mention the whore.
SHELLEY: Gordon!
GORDON: 'But you are, Blanche, you are.' Bette Davis. *What Ever Happened to Baby Jane?* 1962.

> SHELLEY *looks daggers at* GORDON. SCARLETT *starts chopping beside* SHELLEY. *She glances at* SHELLEY *disdainfully.*

SHELLEY: Something wrong?
SCARLETT: No, no.
SHELLEY: We were drunk.

> STEVE *comes back in from the coolroom.*

SCARLETT: [*loudly to* STEVE] Another full house tonight. We should have another party.
SHELLEY: Don't be so bloody judgemental!
SCARLETT: I haven't said a word.
SHELLEY: Why do you think people have parties? So something exciting might happen.
SCARLETT: Something exciting. That's all it was to you?
SHELLEY: [*going out into the restaurant*] We all have brief attacks of lust.
SCARLETT: Yeah, well next time you have one, don't do it in a food preparation area!

> STEVE *looks up again, embarrassed.*

STEVE: Scarlett, I got an email last night from Madeleine, she's coming back. She heard that the restaurant's become a big success.
SCARLETT: You know that's the reason and you're still going to have her back?
STEVE: Scarls, it's complicated. Kids and... and I didn't want to admit it to myself, but there is still some... electricity.
SCARLETT: How's her voltage compared with Shelley?
STEVE: Please, the last thing I need is for her to find out about Shelley.
SCARLETT: Too late. My phone video's on 'YouTube'. Two hundred and fifty thousand hits.
GORDON: A lot of people say they prefer it to Paris Hilton.

> SHELLEY *sweeps in from the restaurant.*

SHELLEY: There's a journalist out there from the *Sun-Herald* who wants to know what date Al Gore was here, how long he was here, what he ate, and when exactly he made the quote you've been using, that it was 'the most unforgettable meal he'd ever had'?

There's a silence. She picks up a local newspaper and thumbs through to the ad section.

SCARLETT: Al Gore? Alan? My Alan?

She's outraged.

STEVE: It was just a joke.
SHELLEY: [*to* STEVE] Didn't you realise that someone would ask questions?
SCARLETT: How could you do this?

There's a silence.

Alan's shy. He'll hate this.

On the screen we see a photograph of a rather startled ALAN *caught by a news photograph in the street. The headline reads: 'The other Al Gore. Rip-off restaurant scam. Fake Al Gore paid thousands to lie.'*

SCENE NINE: AL'S BACK

Two days later, 7.40 p.m. SCARLETT *is about to go out into the restaurant with wine, when* SHELLEY *comes in carrying empty entrée plates.*

SHELLEY: He's out there.
SCARLETT: Alan?
STEVE: Take him champagne. Tell him we're sorry.

SCARLETT *scurries off.*

SHELLEY: Sorry? Business has got even better since the story broke.
GORDON: Count the column inches.
SCARLETT: [*offstage*] There's only Asti spumante, Hardy's sparkling and a few Veuve Cliquots.
STEVE: The spumante. He won't know the difference.
SHELLEY: Steve, that stuff's bottled sugar. My cat wouldn't drink it.
STEVE: Okay. Tell him the meal's on us too.

SCARLETT *goes out to meet* ALAN. *He's got a bandage on his forehead.*

SCARLETT: Alan, I didn't expect to see you back here—What happened?
ALAN: I tripped running away from the paparazzi.

ACT TWO

SCARLETT: I'm so sorry about the Al Gore thing.
ALAN: I wrote that message for you. I wouldn't have ever thought you'd use it like that.
SCARLETT: I didn't, Alan.
ALAN: Yeah, sure.
SCARLETT: I didn't. I showed your message to Steve and he got the idea and I didn't know anything about it.
ALAN: You were just nice to me for the tips.
SCARLETT: No! If I had've known what Steve was up to I would have stopped it. If you don't want to believe that, then fine.
ALAN: You didn't know? You really didn't know?
SCARLETT: I was just as angry as you are. Truly.
ALAN: Truly?
SCARLETT: Truly. I told Steve what I thought of him.
ALAN: Oh, Scar—

> SCARLETT *accidentally sets off the cork from the bottle and hits* ALAN.

SCARLETT: Oh. Sorry.
ALAN: No. I'm okay. You know when you said that you might… when things settle down… watch a movie at your place… *Casablanca* maybe…
SCARLETT: Things are still very hectic.

> ALAN *nods and looks down, mournfully.* SCARLETT *relents.*

Look, it's not really that. I live with my mother.
ALAN: That's fine. I'd like to meet her.
SCARLETT: I don't really think so.
ALAN: Why, what's she like?

> SCARLETT's *film imagination comes up with an immediate answer: The Wicked Witch of the West in* The Wizard of Oz. *On screen the Witch, on her broomstick, circles the tower and flies off with an evil cackle.*

Scarlett?

> SCARLETT *snaps out of it. She shudders.*

SCARLETT: Okay. Let's do it. But be prepared.

> *On screen: John Wayne in* Rooster Cogburn.

JOHN WAYNE: Fill your hands, you son of a bitch.

SCENE TEN: HOME VISIT

Nine days later, 2.15 p.m. SCARLETT *is anxiously tidying up the place.* MAUREEN *pops her head in, smiling.*

SCARLETT: Mum, don't hang around.
MAUREEN: I'll keep right out of the way, dear.
SCARLETT: I've ordered some pizzas. I'll bring yours to your room when they come. Don't hang around.
MAUREEN: Just introduce me and you won't see me again. He's in computers? Makes money?
SCARLETT: Yes. He's just a little bit...
MAUREEN: What?
SCARLETT: Unusual.
MAUREEN: [*alert*] Unusual? In what way unusual?
SCARLETT: He's just a little different.
MAUREEN: He's odd? Is that what you're saying?
SCARLETT: In a nice sort of way.
MAUREEN: How can people be odd in a nice sort of way?
SCARLETT: Just don't grill him. Okay... Say hello, and then out. Please.
MAUREEN: Is he on medication?
SCARLETT: I don't know.
MAUREEN: If he's on antidepressants it can be very dangerous. All those homicidal massacres in America have been linked to antidepressants.
SCARLETT: Don't you dare ask him about anything like that.
MAUREEN: I'm a mother. I've got a right to know. Eva's daughter Romana didn't tell her Kevin had had a vasectomy. She was devastated.

There's a ring at the door. MAUREEN *is wary.*

You're hiding something. I'm going to get to the bottom of this.
SCARLETT: Mum, say hello, then go!

She opens the door. It's ALAN.

Alan? Come in. Ah, this is my mother Maureen.
MAUREEN: Alan, so nice to meet you.
ALAN: Likewise, Mrs O'Hara.
MAUREEN: Scarlett's told me a lot about you.
ALAN: [*trying to joke*] Nothing bad I hope.

ACT TWO

There's a silence. SCARLETT *makes vigorous hand signals that indicate that her mother should go to her room.* MAUREEN *ignores them.*

SCARLETT: Well, Mum, I'll see you in the morning.
MAUREEN: Do you see a lot of your parents?
SCARLETT: Mum, Alan's parents died when he was young.
MAUREEN: That must have been very hard to cope with.
ALAN: It was.
MAUREEN: It happened to a friend of mine. She got very down later in life. Needed antidepressants. Did it ever affect you like that?
SCARLETT: Mum, Alan's just here to see a video.
MAUREEN: You never needed medication?
ALAN: No.
SCARLETT: Mum!
MAUREEN: I'm so glad to hear it. You're one of the lucky ones.
SCARLETT: Mum!
MAUREEN: It's nice you two have met. A mother always lives in hope. Grandchildren, that sort of thing. But that's probably the last thing on your mind.
ALAN: Well, er… one day perhaps.
MAUREEN: Nice that you're thinking that way. You obviously haven't had that little… 'snip'.

SCARLETT *is speechless with horror.* ALAN *is rooted to the spot.*

ALAN: Ah, I think I parked in a no parking zone.

He's out the door and gone.

MAUREEN: I see what you mean. He is odd. I asked a few questions and he ran.
SCARLETT: [*she's lost it*] Who wouldn't if they had to put up with you!
MAUREEN: That's a horrible thing to say!
SCARLETT: I've barely started! You're a bullying old cow! And totally self-obsessed. The whole world's about you! Your aches, your pains, your bloody bone density. Snap like a reed in the wind. See if I care!
MAUREEN: Scarlett.
SCARLETT: The truth is you're not going to snap in any case. I rang Dr Carstairs and he says your bone density readings are perfectly

normal. And everything else about your health is perfectly normal. You're just an evil old…

> *There is a ring at the door.* SCARLETT *looks at her mother menacingly.*

He's back. Sit down and don't you dare mention mental problems.

> *She opens the door.* GARY *is there in a pizza delivery outfit. He looks flabbergasted to see that it's her.*

GARY: Fresh and quick. Our cheese is thick…
SCARLETT: Gary? Aren't you on cable?
GARY: Ah. That's been put on hold for a while. You ordered pizzas?
SCARLETT: Yes, and they better be hot.
GARY: Scarls, I've had to bring them right across the city.
SCARLETT: [*feeling them*] Take them back.
GARY: Gees, Scarls.
SCARLETT: Take them back! No, wait a minute. Don't.

> SCARLETT *takes the cold pizza, dumps it on her mother's head, then storms off to her bedroom.*
>
> *On screen:* The Wizard of Oz, *'Ding Dong, the Witch Is Dead'.*

SCENE ELEVEN: PROPOSAL

Two days later, 7.42 p.m. In the restaurant, GORDON *is cleaning,* STEVE *is doing prep and* SHELLEY *is helping prepare the desserts.* SCARLETT *comes in looking sad. No-one says anything as* SCARLETT *moves across to help with the desserts.* SHELLEY *flashes her hand around as much as she can. It has a huge engagement ring on it. Nobody notices. She finally gets fed up.*

SHELLEY: Well, aren't we all observant today? [*She holds up the ring.*] I'm engaged.
STEVE: [*not interested*] Who to?
SHELLEY: Ian of course.

> *They look at each other and her.*

STEVE: The guy who's the ugly version of Michael Moore?
SHELLEY: He's charming, kind, generous and he's got a BMW and an MBA.

She's obviously miffed that no-one cares or agrees. She sweeps out into the restaurant to check on orders. She comes in again.

Vice-President Gore is back.

> SHELLEY *sweeps out again.* SCARLETT *goes out into the restaurant.* ALAN *is sitting there in his banquette.*

SCARLETT: I'm so, so sorry about what happened.

ALAN: Actually your mother had a point. That's why I'm here.

SCARLETT: [*surprised*] Had a point? You are likely to dismember me in a drug-induced rage?

ALAN: Ah, no, but... I have been seeing a psychologist.

SCARLETT: A what... Alan, I don't understand.

ALAN: [*struggling to say it*] I've got a... er, mild... er, behavioural disorder.

SCARLETT: What do you mean?

ALAN: I'm a social phobic.

SCARLETT: A sorry... a what?

ALAN: Basically that I'm terrified of people.

SCARLETT: But you came to the restaurant... you took me to the zoo...

ALAN: All on the orders of my therapist. It was graded in stages. First I had to go to a restaurant and stay there till I finished my meal. As you might remember that took a few goes. Then I had to try and make someone laugh, then ask someone out to a concert. And finally, be invited home by someone.

SCARLETT: I was just part of a program. Anyone would have done?

ALAN: Well no...

SCARLETT: I just happened to be there?

ALAN: Well yes, but...

SCARLETT: Alan, I think you'd better leave. I have a personality disorder too. I get extremely violent with men who have fucked me over!

ALAN: I just came here to say...

SCARLETT: Alan, I don't want to hear what you've got to say. Go!

> *She walks furiously into the kitchen, accidentally hitting* ALAN *with the door, who in turn hits* SHELLEY *with the back of his head.* SCARLETT *attacks the meat with a tenderiser.* ALAN *enters the kitchen, hitting* GORDON *and then* SHELLEY *with the door, and walks resolutely towards* SCARLETT.

ALAN: No, that's what I've always done. Run.
SCARLETT: Then do it again!
ALAN: [*suddenly fiery and determined*] No, listen. Just listen!

> SCARLETT *is about to tell him to go again, but his passion stops her.*

I didn't have to come back to this restaurant, I could've gone to another, and I didn't have to ask you to a concert, I could have asked anyone. The truth is, the more I saw you the more I wanted to see you. The truth is... [*beat*] I love you.
SCARLETT: [*stunned*] What?
ALAN: I've been too embarrassed all my life to say the things I should have said. Okay, I'm not Humphrey Bogart. I'm not Gary Cooper, Errol Flynn, Clark Gable, John Wayne or Cary Grant... but... Will you marry me?

> GORDON, *absorbed, drops a bowl.*

SCARLETT: Alan, this is not a movie, it's life! I hardly know you.
ALAN: [*fiercely*] 'Now, you listen to me! I don't want any plastics! I don't want any ground floors, and I don't want to get married—ever—to anyone! You understand that? I want to do what I want to do. And you're... and you're...'

> *He pulls her to him in a fierce embrace.*

GORDON: Jimmy Stewart. *It's a Wonderful Life.* 1945.
SCARLETT: Alan, please...
ALAN: 'Don't you pretend nobody ever did that before.'

> ALAN *kisses her again.*

GORDON: Gregory Peck. *Duel in the Sun.* 1946.
ALAN: 'You should be kissed, and often, by somebody who knows how.'

> *He kisses* SCARLETT *again.*

GORDON: Clark Gable. *Gone with the Wind.* 1939.

> SCARLETT *breaks away.*

SCARLETT: Alan, in real life it doesn't work that way.

> *There's a groan from* GORDON.

Shut up, you old poof!
ALAN: [*passionate*] We were built to share our lives with someone. In my case I think it's you. Okay, I'm never going to be the sort of

person who sparkles at dinner parties. I accept that. But at least I've said goodbye to my therapist and at least I've got as far as doing this. If you tell me it's ridiculous…

SCARLETT: I didn't say ridiculous.

ALAN: If you tell me it's never going to be an option…

SCARLETT: I wouldn't say necessarily say never, but…

ALAN: … then I'll go. But, I want to give the real world a try, Scarlett. I want to experience new things. Climb every mountain, forge every stream. Whatever you want to do, I'll do it.

STEVE: Whatever it is, for God's sake, go and do it! I want to get back to business.

SCARLETT: But, Steve, how will you manage without me?

STEVE: I'll cope.

> STEVE *gives* SCARLETT *her bike helmet.*

SHELLEY: [*singing Mendelssohn's 'Wedding March'*] Da da da-da.

> *In a rare moment of fellow feeling,* SHELLEY *gives* SCARLETT *a hug.* SCARLETT *and* SHELLEY*'s earrings get entangled.*

> SCARLETT *takes off her waitress's apron. She takes* ALAN*'s hand, and as they're moving offstage she turns to wave to* GORDON, *gets disorientated, bumps into* ALAN, *then bounces off to collide with* SHELLEY *coming past with plates and the inevitable disaster happens.* GORDON *winces.* SCARLETT *trips over one of the plates.* ALAN *supports her. She smiles at him and they manage to get offstage. But then she's back onstage again running across to* GORDON *to give him a kiss goodbye, which she does before running back offstage.* GORDON *waits for the inevitable and sure enough there's a loud crash as she trips up over something offstage.* GORDON *smiles ruefully.*

GORDON: 'Louis, I think this is the beginning of a beautiful friendship.'

SCARLETT: [*offstage*] Humphrey Bogart. *Casablanca.* 1942.

> *Up on the screen we see the breathless trailer for a forthcoming contemporary movie. The appropriate images of* SCARLETT, ALAN, STEVE, GARY, SHELLEY, GORDON *and* MAUREEN *appear on the screen.*

VOICE-OVER: She was a waitress on the way down…

> *Shots of* SCARLETT *at work, stumbling, spraying cream.*

He was a nerd who couldn't cope...

Shots of a terror stricken ALAN *fleeing.*

The odds were stacked against them...

Shots of them with MAUREEN, SHELLEY, GARY.

But the human heart has a way of making the impossible possible, the unthinkable thinkable, and the evitable inevitable. This is such a story. A heart-warming affirmation that the hunger for romance, embedded deep in the yearning recesses of the human soul, will be with us until the end of time.

The images lead up to wedding shots, with all our main characters there, and MAUREEN *looking marginalised and grumpy. No granny flat for her. Over the top of the marriage imagery we see what the film critics have to say.*

THE END

LET THE SUNSHINE

Foreword

Sandra Bates

What a joy it is to work on a new script by David Williamson and watch its development. He usually writes about ten drafts, honing, refining and updating; adding more humour to some scenes, more poignancy to others. Sometimes there are major changes.

This was the case with *Let The Sunshine*. The first draft took place at Toby's fiftieth birthday party with three couples aged in their late 40s to early 50s. The main protagonists were politically opposed but their offspring didn't appear until draft two, when the third couple disappeared. Even in the first draft though it was a story of the Montagues and the Capulets. So when Romeo and Juliet were placed centre stage the stakes increased considerably.

After polishing the story through subsequent drafts, the script was headed for production when real life interfered in a spectacular fashion: the global economic downturn hit and Barack Obama won the US presidency. David immediately did a massive overhaul and delivered a new manuscript to me.

About six weeks before rehearsals began, we had a reading of the script, after which David made some minor changes. Once rehearsals started early in April 2009, though, I held my breath. The final scene of the play is set in May 2009 and our first preview was 7 May 2009. I did not want any more massive world changes and confess to a huge sigh of relief when the first day of May rolled around, catastrophe-free.

Not that a play is ever set in concrete. After David had seen it a few times with an audience, he adjusted things based on their reaction. For example, Natasha had originally said Rick had 'all the charm of a Pitbull terrier'. Since a small child had recently been mauled and killed by a ferocious dog, there was no way the audience would laugh at this line. At the same time there was an enormous amount in the news about the appalling behaviour of NRL players. David changed the line so that Rick now had 'all the charm of an NRL star on a team bonding weekend'. Kate Raison, who played Natasha only got to 'NRL star' before the audience started hooting with laughter.

This is one of David's greatest skills: his acute powers of observation both when he writes his plays and also in the way he reads the audiences' reaction to them. He writes for us now. Yet while his plays are always timely, the earlier ones speak to us over years. Think of *Don's Party, The Club, Travelling North, The Removalists, Emerald City* and *After The Ball*, to name a few. They do this because they deal with themes, a core of behaviours and truths that have a universality that doesn't date.

While best known for his comedies or satires, it is hard to pin David down to a genre: he has written also dramas, tragedies, biographical plays and issue plays. In fact, not only has he written across genres, he has made up his own. His three conferencing plays—*Face to Face, A Conversation* and *Charitable Intent*—defy the rules of playwriting: they start at the climax and build down to a resolution. And they work so well that many of his admirers declare them to be their favourite Williamson plays.

Similarly, although he is often perceived to write a plethora of one-liners, David's humour is based in the absurdities of our lives, and he often finds comedy in quite painful situations. When actors play their roles truthfully it is clear these supposed one liners are inherent to the story. The stronger the emotion—be it pain anger or jealousy—and the higher the stakes, the funnier or more poignant the lines become. We identify with the characters and react accordingly because we're sitting with them on the rollercoaster. Certainly this was the case with the original cast of *Let The Sunshine* who took their audiences on a wonderful journey.

If you are reading or studying *Let The Sunshine*, I hope you enjoy it as much as we have. If there isn't a production on while you are studying it, why not try and stage it yourselves? Plays are written to be performed—it's the collaborative effort of everyone involved that makes it so rewarding, such fun. You'll be delighted how much more you get from it, even if you simply read it out loud amongst yourselves.

And you'll also discover for yourselves how privileged we are to have a playwright of the calibre of David Williamson writing for us, about us, right now.

Sandra Bates
Artistic and Governing Director, Ensemble Theatre
June 2009

Let the Sunshine was first produced by Ensemble Theatre at Ensemble Theatre, Kirribilli, on 7 May 2009, with the following cast:

TOBY	William Zappa
ROS	Georgie Parker
RICK	Justin Stewart Cotta
RON	Andrew McFarlane
NATASHA	Kate Raison
EMMA	Emma Jackson

Director, Sandra Bates
Designer, Graham Maclean
Lighting designer, Matthew Marshall

CHARACTERS

TOBY, 60. A producer/director of hard-hitting left-leaning documentaries. Anxious, truculent, vulnerable.

ROS, mid 50s. His wife. Successful publishing career, now a freelance editor. Calmer, more resilient than her husband, but don't mess with her.

RICK, 30. Their son. Never academic, he's obsessed with music and trying to make it as a songwriter/performer. Anxious about his future, wryly funny, and generous of spirit, but not without ambition. More than a touch of steel under the laid-back surface.

RON, late 50s. A hugely wealthy property developer who has very pronounced right-wing views. He fancies himself as a ladies man and hates dole bludgers and indolence.

NATASHA, late 50s. His wife. She's the queen bee of Noosa. She knows everyone who counts in town and leads an active social life. She dabbled with a business career but got tired of it. But she's no fool, especially when it comes to sensing that her social pre-eminence might be under challenge.

EMMA, 34. Their daughter. Described in the play as a Mack truck without brakes, she's a driven and successful corporate lawyer. But she's at the crossroads. Career or motherhood. Under the toughness there's still vulnerability.

ACT ONE

March 2007.

TOBY *is fitting together a bookshelf that he's bought from Ikea. He's having a lot of trouble. He was never much good at reading instructions and he's cursing quietly to himself as the pieces stubbornly refuse to fit together. His wife* ROS *enters with an armful of books, obviously expecting there to have been much more progress than has actually been made.*

TOBY: [*indicating the pieces*] Why do we need this bloody thing?
ROS: [*indicating the books*] Because you keep buying books you never read.
TOBY: I do read them.
ROS: [*reading a title*] *The Selfish Gene.* Richard Dawkins.
TOBY: Hugely important. It was the final nail in the coffin of any thought we were fashioned in God's image.
ROS: What does it say?
TOBY: That like every other animal we're a biological survival machine constructed by our genes. The genes that survive are the ones that help make good survival machines.
ROS: Survival machines? We're survival machines? Nothing more?
TOBY: Every one of your ancestors, from way back to the amoeba, survived and reproduced.
ROS: Toby, that's a ghastly level of reductionism.
TOBY: [*with a shrug*] I'm not ashamed to own up to the amoeba in me.
ROS: It *is* more obvious in you. [*Looking at the date of publication*] Published 1976? You read it back then?
TOBY: Yes.
ROS: If it's that important, how come you've never mentioned it?
TOBY: For the same reason I kept my porn magazines at the back of my filing cabinet. To avoid a messy divorce.
ROS: You had porn magazines?
TOBY: I threw them out when I matured.
ROS: Which was when?

TOBY: Oh, er, well over… [*thinking*] … a year ago.

ROS *isn't impressed.*

ROS: [*still holding the book*] Dawkins sole contribution to human thought is that we're survival machines?

TOBY: Yeah, and that millions of years of survival have made us selfish, virulently tribal, deeply competitive and amazingly irrational. Religious fanaticism being the most depressing example of the latter.

ROS: There's no such thing as compassion, empathy and friendship?

TOBY: [*with a shrug*] Human nature is like a curate's egg. The good parts are very good, but the bad parts can be very bad indeed. Bad enough to put an end to any thought that 'Peace shall rule the planets, and love will steer the stars'.

ROS: It's such fun being married to you. What do you want to do for your birthday?

TOBY: Nothing.

ROS: You're about to turn sixty.

TOBY: Which is why I want to do nothing.

ROS: [*putting down the books*] You have to do something. You're becoming a social isolate.

TOBY: Do what?

ROS: Perhaps a little dinner out. With a few friends.

TOBY: I haven't got any.

ROS: Ron and Natasha?

TOBY: Natasha? The cosmetically-enhanced smiling piranha?

ROS: All right. Just a thought.

TOBY: And High-Rise Ron?

ROS: All right, he's a developer, but—

TOBY: The dentist told me they call him 'The Magician'. With the wave of a brown paper bag he can turn rural zoning to residential.

ROS: It's pretty sad. We've been here over a year and you've got absolutely no friends.

TOBY: I've got friends. It's just they're all in Sydney.

ROS: Not since that 'forthright' *SMH* interview, in which you said Sydney was full of pretentious elitist wankers.

TOBY: It is. If I was asked to name the two most boring two hours of my life it would be listening to Sacha rabbit on about Byambasuren Davaa.

ROS: Who?

TOBY: How could you have forgotten? The Mongolian filmmaker who explored, apparently at a very slow pace, the family dynamics of life in a yurt.

ROS: You made that up.

TOBY: Google him. And there were hundreds even more obscure.

ROS: All right. Forget the birthday dinner.

TOBY: I hate this place. Let's go and live somewhere else.

ROS: You drag me up here against my will and now you hate it?

TOBY: When I used to come here thirty-five years ago it was a beautiful little fishing village. Now the only growth industry is plastic surgery. Let's go to Tasmania.

ROS: And wear thermal underwear ten months of the year?

TOBY: Melbourne.

ROS: Melbourne?

TOBY: Coffee lounges, wine bars, dinner parties, political arguments…

ROS: Thermal underwear eight months a year.

TOBY: Cold is bracing. They have seasons.

ROS: No! I grieved for Sydney for a year, but I've got used to it here.

TOBY: Wouldn't you like to be somewhere authentic? Somewhere where you aren't blinded by the dazzle of gold jewellery every time you hit Hastings Street? [*He thinks.*] Byron Bay.

ROS: Byron Bay? Authentic? Like Las Vegas is tasteful?

TOBY: At least there's some chance you might meet someone who voted Labor twenty years ago.

ROS: I like it here now.

TOBY: You like it?

ROS: It's beautiful, far less stressful than Sydney, the climate's great and it's a very healthy lifestyle.

TOBY: The mind? Where is the food for the mind? The main topic of conversation here is whether schnauzers are better house dogs than miniature poodles.

ROS: I'm getting as much consulting work as I want and it's a great place to work.

TOBY: Great place for you.

ROS: You'd be far less miserable if you spent a bit of time making friends *here*. Go out and have lunch with some guys.

TOBY: And talk about what?

ROS: How you feel about life?

TOBY: I know how I feel about life. Absolutely shithouse.

ROS: Turning sixty is a milestone. You can't just let it pass.

TOBY: Okay, We'll go out with your old school friend Natasha, and *Ron*. But you call them. Please. You can always work out what people are really saying. I always stuff it up.

ROS: [*hesitating then sighing: okay*] What restaurant?

TOBY: You choose.

ROS: It's your birthday. You can go where you like.

TOBY: You know and I know we're going to end up going where you want to go. Choose the venue, and call them.

ROS: [*pointing to a piece of the bookcase*] That should go round the other way, shouldn't it?

> *She walks out.* TOBY *looks at the piece, picks it up, tries it out and, to his annoyance, his wife was right.*
>
> RON, *fifties, dressed casually but stylishly, sits watching cricket on television.* NATASHA, *very slim, attractive and chic, enters.*

NATASHA: Cricket? Again?

> RON *stares at the screen and doesn't answer.*

Ron.

RON: [*irritated, motioning her to shut up*] He's just about to get his hundred. [*Sudden horror*] No. No. No. Oh, shit!

NATASHA: What?

RON: Caught on the boundary. Ninety-nine. He's going to be suicidal.

NATASHA: He and I both.

RON: [*looking at the screen*] Look at that bloody Indian doing cartwheels. [*He shouts at the screen.*] Look at him. Prancing around like a turbaned chimpanzee. If I was racist, the race I'd hate most would be bloody Indians.

> *He looks at* NATASHA *who is still waiting.*

What?

NATASHA: When we're out you're always Mr Charm. I wish they could see you at home.

RON: What?

NATASHA: Ros rang. She wants us to go to a birthday dinner for Toby.

ACT ONE

RON: Okay.

NATASHA: You want to go?

RON: No, he's a self-righteous prick.

NATASHA: We can think of an excuse.

RON: Ros is okay.

NATASHA: I think everybody realises you think Ros is okay.

RON: You have to admit she looks great for her age. Do you think she's had a bit of knife work too?

NATASHA: If we do go out with them, please don't give her any more neck rubs.

RON: With a miserable husband like that, she needs them.

NATASHA: We've got an excuse. Emma is coming.

RON: It'd be hard to explain why we can't take one night off when Emma's coming for a week. Why is she coming for a week?

NATASHA: She's going to be made a partner.

RON: At her age? That's amazing.

NATASHA: I think she wants us to know. Or more particularly, you to know.

RON: She doesn't care what I think.

NATASHA: The reason she always came top of the class was because it was the only time you ever praised her.

RON: If she cares what I think, why does she give me such a hard time?

NATASHA: Because she had to try so hard to get you to notice her.

RON: That mouth of hers is a lethal weapon.

NATASHA: When she gets here just don't keep grilling her about her private life.

RON: I didn't know she had one.

NATASHA: It's hard to have a social life working eighty hours a week.

RON: How many guys has she split up with now? I've lost count.

NATASHA: It's her life. Try and be accepting.

RON: I introduced her to at least three young men who are on their way to becoming seriously wealthy and she wouldn't date any of them.

NATASHA: She is on her way to becoming seriously wealthy herself.

RON: Young Simon Marsh was besotted with her and he's well into six figures already.

NATASHA: Yes, around his waistline. She's not interested in accountants.

RON: Who is she interested in? Guys like that useless sod who worked as a greenkeeper and called himself a poet?

NATASHA: She likes men who are creative.
RON: Simon is the most creative accountant in the country. That's why he earns a fortune.
NATASHA: She's not going to marry an overweight balding accountant.
RON: Who will she marry?
NATASHA: She may not marry anyone.
RON: [*frowning*] What?
NATASHA: It's possible she's not that way inclined.
RON: What are you talking about?
NATASHA: She's grown very fond of Sammy.
RON: That girl she flats with?
NATASHA: Yes.
RON: She told you that?
NATASHA: I've been picking up signals.
RON: Our daughter's climbing on top of other women and you just accept it?
NATASHA: I might be wrong.
RON: Well, I'm sorry. I'm not like those gooey parents who say, 'If my son wants to play the "Dance of the Sugar Plum Fairies" and dance around the living room in a tutu, I couldn't be happier'.
NATASHA: Everyone in her generation tries things. When she gets here, do *not* interrogate her.
RON: Me? Interrogate our daughter? That's like telling a cocker spaniel to go easy on a rottweiler.
NATASHA: What do you want? An adoring little doormat who approves of everything you do?
RON: Yes. Where do I find one?
NATASHA: It's not going to happen.
RON: Sammy? She's not even all that attractive?
NATASHA: I may be wrong. Can you get your mind back on what we are going to do about this dinner out with Toby and Ros?
RON: We'll go. Ros is nice.
NATASHA: You don't have to go through a book club meeting with her.
RON: What's the problem?
NATASHA: Every time she opens her mouth it's always 'Sydney this, Sydney that'. 'Or as my famous author friend Geraldine Brooks said…'

ACT ONE

RON: Who's Geraldine Brooks?
NATASHA: She only won a Pulitzer Prize. Why don't you occasionally read something other than the *Financial Review*?
RON: I'm sorry I've wasted my life amassing a fortune.
NATASHA: Money's not the only thing that sustains human life.
RON: It's third after air and water.
NATASHA: This is only Ros's 'default' book club. She goes down to her 'real' book club in Sydney once a month so she can experience 'real' literary debate. Let's not go to this damned birthday.

RON's attention is caught by the screen again.

RON: [*shrieking in delight*] Six! Couldn't catch that one, could you? You star, Ricky! Knock his greasy turban off.

NATASHA sighs. She leaves.

ROS enters the living room where TOBY has finally got the bookshelf together and is standing and gazing at it with immense pride. He turns to her, beaming and indicates it.

ROS: Amazing. Now you can put those books in.
TOBY: [*staring at it*] I think I got more pleasure out of that than the last few films I made.
ROS: They can't come.
TOBY: Change the date.
ROS: I did. I gave several alternatives. They still can't come.
TOBY: [*with a surge of anger*] They don't want to come.
ROS: Perhaps because last time you picked a fight on every possible occasion.
TOBY: I've been nominated for the Academy Award twice, and they can't even be bothered coming.
ROS: Yes, that *is* odd. Most people would feel honoured to be insulted by a double nominee.
TOBY: I've got a drawer full of letters from people I've never met who'd love to have dinner with me.
ROS: Write and offer to fly them up here.
TOBY: Who does Ron think he is? Okay, he's obscenely wealthy, and women throw themselves at him because he lays on the charm like a trowel, but what's he got apart from that?
ROS: [*shrugging in agreement*] Apart from wealth and charm, nothing.

TOBY: My life has amounted to more than using rat cunning to turn the most beautiful coastline in Australia into an architectural abomination!
ROS: Natasha said he's using prize-winning architects.
TOBY: What prize? Best Tuscan villa imitations in South-East Queensland? I gave them a box set of my documentaries and they haven't even bothered to watch one.
ROS: I'm not sure that the message that Western capitalism is sick at its core resonates all that well in Noosa.
TOBY: [*suddenly insecure*] My life *has* amounted to something, hasn't it? Up here where money is God, I start to wonder.
ROS: Your work is fine, but *you* are difficult.
TOBY: Me?
ROS: Yes you.
TOBY: You've never said that before.
ROS: You've never been as difficult before.
TOBY: Have I got that bad?
ROS: Yes.
TOBY: I'm on edge at the moment. The German money is wavering. I'm sorry I'm not much fun to be with. It's nothing to do with how I feel about you.
ROS: If I thought it was I'd be out of here.
TOBY: Don't say that. Please. That's my worst nightmare. I wake up in the morning and you've gone.
ROS: I have to say I've been doing quite a bit of mental packing lately.
TOBY: Don't say that. I'm crazy about you.
ROS: I'd never have known.
TOBY: Surely it's obvious at some level.
ROS: At no level.
TOBY: Sometimes I'll see you at the other end of a room, or walking to the car, and after all these years, I still find myself feeling this incredible… warmth and… pride. Almost like… tears-of-joy territory, and thank whoever that we ended up together. Surely you know that.
ROS: I didn't, but it's nice to hear it. [*Hesitating, then hugging him*] I guess that's why I'm still here.
TOBY: I'm sorry I dragged you up here. I had to get out of Sydney. I felt totally humiliated.

ROS: You trusted your sources and one of them was a liar. It didn't mean your whole film was wrong. Multinationals do exploit Third-World workers.

TOBY: That stuff-up gave the right-wing press the opportunity they'd been waiting for for years.

ROS: What the film was saying wasn't wrong.

TOBY: I should have double-checked. In my business you've got to get everything right. Everything.

ROS: Let's just go out together on your birthday.

TOBY: I'm on first name terms with Al Gore and those two arseholes cut me dead.

> ROS *is on the phone to* RICK, *her son. A good-looking young man of thirty dressed like a rock musician, which he is. He may appear to be laid-back but there's a latent steeliness under that manner.*

ROS: Have you done the demo tape yet?

RICK: I'm not sure the songs are quite ready.

ROS: What do the other guys think?

RICK: Yeah, they sort of think they're fine, but I'm not sure.

ROS: Why not try and see how it goes?

RICK: I want one song on there that's so good that everyone just goes 'Wow'.

ROS: That one you played me when I was down there was *great*.

RICK: Thanks, Mum, but I have to go up a notch.

ROS: Have you found a good producer yet?

RICK: The ones I can afford are ratshit. I'll probably do it myself.

ROS: If I gave you some cash—

RICK: Mum, you've helped me enough.

ROS: That audition for the club gig? How did it go?

RICK: Ummm. Yeah, not bad. Not bad at all.

ROS: Were they impressed?

RICK: Seemed to be. But I decided I didn't want to spend my life doing covers in a third-rate booze club.

ROS: You're sure you're okay? We worry about you.

RICK: I'm fine.

ROS: Still working at that hotel?

RICK: Yeah.

ROS: We get worried.
RICK: Mum, I'm all right.
ROS: If a little more money would make the difference…
RICK: No more. I mean it.
ROS: I've got your account number. I'm only too happy to put some in.
RICK: I'm thirty. You've done enough.
ROS: Are you eating properly?
RICK: [*wearily*] Yes I am.
ROS: What?
RICK: [*what she wants to hear*] Pasta, vegetables, fruit and rice.
ROS: Are you still…?
RICK: Alcohol is right down, the E's… just now and then. The good thing about poverty is that it forces you to live a very healthy lifestyle.
ROS: And the… gunja?
RICK: Mum, leave me with *something*.
ROS: I was going to ask you a favour.
RICK: Yeah?
ROS: Your father's feeling pretty low at the moment. The money for his latest project is proving difficult and… it's his birthday… and he's got absolutely no friends.
RICK: Of course he hasn't. They're all bloody capo bastards up there.
ROS: Not all.
RICK: NoosVegas. Six bucks for coffee in Hastings Street. You've got to be joking.
ROS: Could you come up and surprise him?
RICK: He's really down?
ROS: Yes he is. To quite a worrying degree.
RICK: Okay, I'll come. I've just finished a new song.
ROS: Great. Play it for us when you come up.

    NATASHA *is having coffee with* ROS.

I know Toby can be a bit domineering at times, but I honestly didn't think he was all that bad last time we were together.
NATASHA: Ros, I don't disagree with everything your husband believes, but it's his manner.
ROS: Ron wasn't exactly lost for words either.
NATASHA: If someone challenges him, he's not the sort to back down.

ROS: Toby doesn't suffer fools gladly. [*Realising her gaffe*] Sorry, I'm not implying that Ron is a fool.

NATASHA: Fools aren't generally worth over two hundred million dollars.

ROS: Two hundred million?

NATASHA: Ron's no fool. And being a developer doesn't necessarily mean someone's the antichrist. We can't all just return to nature.

ROS: Let's not discuss this now.

NATASHA: One of the documentaries Toby sent us is called *The Rape of Australia's Coastline*. Maybe that was a little insensitive?

ROS: Terrible things *have* happened. The Gold Coast..

NATASHA: Ron's developments are environmentally sensitive. He says these days you sell more that way. A smaller carbon footprint makes doctors' wives feel good.

ROS: Look, about his birthday…

NATASHA: Why would he want to go out with us in any case? He and Ron obviously have nothing in common.

ROS: Actually, Toby was impressed at Ron's interest in Roman history.

NATASHA: He loves all the treachery and backstabbing. Says it's just like business.

ROS: I'm sure they'll find more things in common.

NATASHA: [*relenting*] It's just a question of when we can do it. I've got a Friends of the Art Gallery committee meeting Tuesday and we're seeing friends every other night, and our daughter Emma's coming up on the weekend.

ROS: Our son Rick's coming up too.

NATASHA: Perhaps they could both come along. It might help keep everyone calm and civil.

Later. TOBY *is on the phone. He's incredulous. Furious. Passionate.*

TOBY: But why? Last time I spoke to Gunther he was absolutely sure the German money was there. [*He can't believe what he's hearing.*] Jewish sensitivities? It's about seventy years too late for the Germans to be worrying about Jewish sensitivities! [*He listens.*] The film will be looking at the human plight of the Palestinians, it's *not* going to be anti-Israel. I'll get onto Gunther and find out exactly what is going on.

He hangs up and sits there staring into space. ROS *enters.*

The film's dead. The Germans have pulled out their money.

ROS: No. Why?

TOBY: The Jewish lobby. Even here in Australia they've got five thousand letter writers on instant call if anyone suggests Israel isn't the bravest, most caring, most reasonable nation on earth.

ROS: The film's really finished?

TOBY: I'll fight as hard as I can, but frankly my chances are close to zilch.

ROS: I'm really sorry. You've been passionate about this for so long.

TOBY: Two years in the setting-up. Finished overnight.

ROS: I'm really sorry.

TOBY: Frankly, I'd counted on the money.

ROS: Don't worry.

TOBY: All I get for those two years is that dribble of development cash.

ROS: We're fine. The last three books I commissioned have been going gangbusters.

TOBY: The family finances shouldn't have to rely on you.

TOBY *shakes his head mournfully.*

ROS: Ah, Natasha and Ron have found a free evening in their incredibly crowded social calendar, and would like to celebrate your birthday with us.

TOBY *looks at her suspiciously.*

TOBY: Suddenly?

ROS: Yes.

TOBY: You spoke to Natasha.

ROS: No.

TOBY: You're lying.

ROS: Yes I am. I had coffee with Natasha who, by the way, says she often agrees with what you say.

TOBY: You're kidding.

ROS: No, she told me.

TOBY: She always did strike me as a lot brighter than her husband.

ROS: Your birthday dinner is next Tuesday at Coconut Grove.

TOBY: Isn't that the most expensive restaurant in town?

ROS: No.

ACT ONE

TOBY: Isn't it the one where there's no wine under sixty dollars?

ROS: No. It's reasonable and it's the best food and atmosphere in town.

TOBY: Well, we're not having wine from the top end of the list. Not now the Germans have pulled out.

ROS: Don't embarrass me by ordering the cheapest.

TOBY: Second cheapest is usually fine.

ROS: Third cheapest. And don't...

TOBY: What?

ROS: Pick fights.

TOBY: [*outraged*] Pick fights? Having discussions about the most important issues facing our planet is picking fights?

ROS: [*getting irritated*] You know and I know that it's no use arguing issues with Ron. You're not going to change him.

TOBY: 'You're absolutely right, Ron. What we should be aiming for is low tax, zero welfare, high profit, cheap labour, and the kind of widening inequalities which reflect the fact that most people are idiots and get what they deserve.' Why in the hell are we going out with them?

ROS: [*getting really irritated*] Okay, we won't. [*Beat.*] Toby, there is a place in the universe for swapping yarns. For jokes. For simple fun. And it's been a long time since I've experienced any of that.

TOBY: All right. We'll go.

ROS: We're going for a drink at Ron's place before we go to Coconut Grove.

TOBY: Ron's place. Why Ron's place? It's my birthday.

ROS: They're *trying* to be hospitable.

TOBY: Probably got a new Geoffrey Smart painting they want to show off.

ROS: You want to call off the drinks?

TOBY: I guess the evening will pass faster if I'm totally plastered.

ROS: Just lighten up a little bit. Occasionally. Try and relax and have fun.

> *She sighs, not confident that this will happen, as* TOBY *sighs and reluctantly nods his head.*
>
> *A week later.* NATASHA *and* RON *are with their daughter* EMMA. *She's very fashionably dressed. She speaks rapidly and with authority.* RON *is trying to look interested,* NATASHA *is trying not to nod off to sleep.*

EMMA: The big question these days with Mergers and Acquisitions is whether to buy the assets of a company or the company itself. When tax consolidation came in it became a whole new ball game. It's vital now to take into account that there is the potential for the target entity to be liable for the tax obligations of the entire vendor group. The potential liability of the target made a lot of lawyers think that acquisitions had to occur by way of asset sale. But they were wrong for quite a few reasons. First, an asset acquisition often means higher stamp duty—

> NATASHA *can't stop herself nodding off to sleep.* EMMA *sees this and her eyes narrow.*

Mum, if this is boring you, tell me.

NATASHA: No, no. It's just that we've been going out a lot.

EMMA: You asked me what's happening in my job, but if you don't really want to know then don't pretend you do.

NATASHA: No, no. I do. I did a double session of water aerobics this morning.

EMMA: I mean we're talking tens of millions of dollars here. If I make a mistake the implications both for the client, and for me, can be enormous.

RON: It's a huge responsibility. We're both very proud of you.

NATASHA: I can't believe how quickly you've risen in that firm.

RON: And what they pay you.

EMMA: They pay me that because I make money for them.

RON: Being made a partner at your age is extraordinary. Especially for a woman.

EMMA: Dad! I'm not a partner yet. I hope both of you haven't told anyone that it might be happening.

NATASHA: No, no.

EMMA: If anyone at my firm hears that it's on the cards there'll be a lot of hostility.

RON: We haven't mentioned it to anyone.

NATASHA: Hostility? It doesn't sound like a very pleasant working environment.

EMMA: You don't join a top law firm hoping to be drowned in the milk of human kindness. I'm not even sure I want it.

RON: Of course you want it.

NATASHA: Listen to your daughter, Ron. If she's hesitating there may be a reason.
RON: For God's sake, she's worked for years for this.
NATASHA: [*to* EMMA] Frankly, I worry about how can you stay healthy with the hours you work. If I didn't walk in the national park every morning and do my yoga and have my massages, I—
EMMA: That's fine for you, Mother. My generation can't do the lady of leisure thing anymore.
NATASHA: [*irritated*] Lady of leisure? There wasn't much leisure when you were growing up.
RON: Your mother was the best mother you could have had. You weren't an easy child.
EMMA: How would you know? You were never there.
NATASHA: I wasn't *just* a mother. I ran a very successful fashion boutique.
EMMA: For three years and then got bored.
RON: Four years and she sold it for a healthy profit. Well, not so healthy actually, but…

He shrugs.

EMMA: Our generation can't be dilettantes.
NATASHA: Dilettante?
EMMA: It's just as much dog eat dog for women as it is for men these days. You work hard or you bomb out. There are no other options.
NATASHA: Getting married and having kids is still not against the law the last time I checked.
EMMA: I enjoy using my brain.
NATASHA: Define the characteristics that make Dostoyevsky a great novelist?
EMMA: When I use *my* brain, I get paid for it.
RON: The Roman Empire collapsed because its intelligent women didn't breed.
EMMA: Because their husbands' sperm was being redirected into slaves of both sexes.
RON: Okay. Successful, lonely, childless, it's your choice.
EMMA: If some women feel that screaming at their offspring in shopping malls adds deep layers of meaning to their lives, good luck to them.
RON: Parenthood has its occasional stressful moments.

NATASHA: None of which you were ever around to witness.
RON: Most children are delightful most of the time.
EMMA: Dad, every two-year-old I've ever seen is a midget psychopath.
RON: So what you're telling us is no grandchildren?
EMMA: Where exactly do I find a father for these hypotheticals?
RON: I've already introduced you to—
EMMA: Dad, those guys would make a zombie seem hyperactive.
RON: Okay, solid, dependable isn't your thing. You want to walk the flaky side then don't expect commitment.
NATASHA: Darling, I'm sure you could find someone who'll commit.
EMMA: Mum, the thing that most strikes terror into contemporary males is the sight of a bugaboo pram.
NATASHA: Darling, you're intelligent, wealthy—
EMMA: And maybe even a *tiny* bit attractive?
NATASHA: That goes without saying.
EMMA: It usually goes without saying by the men I date too.
RON: Frankly, Emma, you are pretty full-on. If I was a young man you'd scare the tits off me.
EMMA: Thanks.
RON: Well, for God's sake, lighten up a bit sometimes. When a man says something funny, laugh.
EMMA: If it ever happens, I will.
RON: You're too demanding. You start going out with someone and it's over a few months later.
NATASHA: A few weeks later.
RON: Do men just leave you cold? Is there something you're not telling us?

> RON *sneaks a glance at* NATASHA. EMMA *sees the glance and frowns, puzzled.*

If you've got orientation problems I'd like to know about it.
EMMA: Orientation problems? [*She looks suspiciously at her mother.*] What have you been telling him?
NATASHA: [*guiltily*] Nothing.
EMMA: Mum, if I tell you something in confidence, I mean it.
NATASHA: I just told your father you were… getting on well with your flatmate.
EMMA: Oh migod, Mum, if you can't be trusted to—

ACT ONE

NATASHA: It's all I said. Truly, it's all I said.
RON: It's all she said.
EMMA: [*to* RON] So you assumed Sammy and I were going to bed together?
RON: No, no.
EMMA: Well, we did. But it was yuk. She's moved out.
RON: I'm...
EMMA: You're what?
RON: Relieved. Have you got a new flatmate?
EMMA: Yes, Hildegarde. She's a committee member of Dykes on Bikes.

    RON *and* NATASHA *look at each other.*

Joke, Dad. Joke.
RON: [*laughing nervously*] Hildegarde.
NATASHA: Have you got someone else. Sharing?
EMMA: No. I worked out I'm making enough money not to have to any more.
NATASHA: Isn't that a little lonely?
EMMA: It's great. I don't have to pretend to be pleasant when I'm in a foul mood, and I can watch *my* DVDs and listen to *my* music and do things exactly the way I want to do them.
NATASHA: Yes, but aren't you a bit lonely?
EMMA: No.
RON: Well. You seem to have everything worked out in life.
EMMA: Was that some kind of put-down?
RON: No, no.
EMMA: Look, I appreciate your concerns. I do. But I'm a big girl and I'll work out what direction I want my life to take myself. I'll go and change.
NATASHA: Emma, I'm sorry to have to spring this on you, but we've got to go out tomorrow with another couple, but we'd very much like you to come and meet them.
EMMA: [*suspicious*] Not that anorexic tart with brown scaly skin and the breast implants that failed?
NATASHA: No.
EMMA: When she's got all her jewellery on she's barely got the strength to stand up.
NATASHA: No, these are new people. Very interesting. He's a documentary filmmaker. Toby Callaghan. You might have heard of him.

EMMA: Is he the one that makes those preachy left-wing sagas full of fake compassion about Third World poverty?

NATASHA: Perhaps you shouldn't come.

RON: No, come. Give it to him. I'm going to if he starts any of his lefty shit.

NATASHA: [*alarmed*] Ron, he's promised to be on his best behaviour. This is a birthday dinner, not a slugfest.

EMMA: That graveyard voice to camera. I can't stand him. Nanny-state leftists! Why on earth would you want to go out with him?

NATASHA: His wife's an old school friend from Melbourne. Well, not actually a friend, she was a year below me. She was in the debating team and ran the school magazine. Thought she was just terrific. Still do.

RON: She's nice.

NATASHA: You know your father. God's gift to women of all sizes, ages and intelligence levels.

EMMA: [*wrinkling up her face*] Not still! Dad, if you only knew how embarrassing and how 'yesterday' all that sexist smarm is you'd stop it immediately.

RON: For God's sake, a touch of innocent flirting. Women still like being noticed.

NATASHA: That doesn't include taking a photo of her in a bathing suit and photo-shopping her legs to make them look longer.

EMMA: Just think for once how embarrassing it is for Mum.

RON: I've never cheated on your mother once in our lives. Ask her if it's the same for her.

NATASHA: Oh, for God's sake. Once. Don't bring this up.

EMMA: Really? Make my day by telling me it happened nine months before I was born.

RON: Bloody personal trainer. We all know which room in the house the training was happening in.

NATASHA: Once. Years and years ago.

EMMA: [*shuddering at the thought*] Move on please. Do you want me to come to this dinner or not?

RON: Yes.

NATASHA: Not if you're hell bent on picking a fight.

RON: Only if he starts it.

ACT ONE

EMMA: Mum, don't be so wishy-washy. If people have stupid ideas they deserve to have them challenged.

RON: Exactly. I'm really glad you're coming. I'd like that prick to see that some people have successful kids. His son's a druggie muso.

EMMA: The son won't be there?

NATASHA: Well, er, yes.

EMMA: No way! If there's one thing I can't stand it's men who pretend they've got talent nobody has been smart enough to discover.

> TOBY *and* ROS *are listening to* RICK, *playing a CD of his latest song. He's clearly talented and it's good, with intelligent lyrics, a good melody line and interesting chord structure. It's reminiscent of Tim Freedman. The music stops.* TOBY *is delighted. He bounds up and embraces his son.*

TOBY: That's terrific.

RICK: [*unsure*] You think?

TOBY: Your stuff's just getting better and better.

ROS: It's really good.

RICK: I'm not sure whether it's got enough… bite.

TOBY: For God's sake, mate. Don't keep putting yourself down. It's brilliant. You should be getting that out to record companies.

RICK: Yeah, maybe.

TOBY: It's fantastic, don't you think, Ros?

ROS: It's very good.

> *She embraces* RICK *too.* RICK *is very pleased but still unsure.*

RICK: It's great to see you guys.

TOBY: It was great that you came up. It was a total surprise.

RICK: Glad to be here.

ROS: I hope you don't mind coming out with us tonight.

RICK: Who are these people?

ROS: It's all a bit of a mistake. She's an old school friend… well actually not really a friend. She was a year above me and hardly spoke to me. She was in the parties, boys, hairstyle, make-up and gossip group.

RICK: You guys go. I'll stay here.

ROS: Their daughter's coming and they'd like you there.

RICK: Their daughter? How old is she?

ROS: In her mid thirties.

RICK: What's she do?

TOBY: From what I hear she's a killing machine.
ROS: She's a corporate lawyer.
RICK: You are kidding. Why are they bringing her?
TOBY: No doubt to show us what a brilliant prodigy they have spawned.
RICK: As distinct from me.
TOBY: You're worth ten of her. Don't keep putting yourself down.
ROS: She could turn out to be interesting.
RICK: A lawyer? If we've got to meet these God-awful people, let's have a drink or two first.
TOBY: Bloody good idea.
RICK: What are their names?
ROS: Emma, Ron and Natasha.
RICK: Which one's the lawyer?
ROS: Emma. Natasha's the mother. At school she was Jocelyn. Then she saw Audrey Hepburn in *War and Peace* and suddenly she was Natasha.
RICK: And Ron.
TOBY: Ron. The perfect name for a property developer. He's apparently worth two hundred million.

> TOBY *opens a bottle of wine. It's screwtop so it's easy and he's soon pouring it.*

RICK: Two hundred million? How did he get that rich?
TOBY: You take one of the world's most beautiful coastlines and turn it to shit.
RICK: Two hundred million? His daughter's starting to sound a little more interesting.
ROS: Rick.
RICK: Joking, Mum. Joking. I learned my lesson about lawyers when I dated one three years ago.
ROS: You didn't tell me about that.
RICK: It was very short. I worked out after two days that no matter what she did she was always going to be able to prove she was right.
TOBY: Son, that's not just lawyers, it's common to the whole female species.

> RICK *takes a generous glass of wine that his father has poured as* TOBY *helps himself to one.*

ROS: Don't drink too much. Either of you. And, Toby, this time no politics.

RICK: Did it get a bit full-on, Dad?
TOBY: Did it ever. I'll tell you some of the things they said—
ROS: Toby, no. You'll rev yourself up again.

> TOBY *tosses back his drink, as does* RICK, *then* TOBY *pours another for the both of them.*

That's the last one. Really. I mean it.

> *Across at the other residence,* NATASHA, RON *and* EMMA *have wine glasses in their hands as they wait for the arrival of their guests.* NATASHA *looks at her watch.* RON *sees her doing it.*

RON: You didn't think they'd be on time?
NATASHA: I didn't think they'd be this late. We'll never get to the restaurant.
RON: Lateness is no accident. It's a sign of contempt.
EMMA: Pour me another drink, Dad.
NATASHA: Emma, isn't that enough?
EMMA: It's a holiday. I'm relaxing.

> RON *pours her another drink. She takes a large mouthful.*

NATASHA: Sounds like them now.

> *She goes off to get the door.*

RON: Prepare to be lectured to.
EMMA: Just let him try.

> TOBY, RICK *and* ROS *enter with* NATASHA. ROS *is looking a little nervous.* TOBY *is trying his best to smile.* RON *advances on* ROS.

RON: I can't believe it. Every time I see you you get more beautiful. Those eyes. If I wasn't married to the most beautiful woman in the world, I'd be down on my knees.

> *He gives her an effusive embrace and kiss on both cheeks.*

EMMA: Dad, will you stop that shit.
RON: What?
EMMA: That!
RON: Emma, lighten up. There's a bit of the peacock in every male.
EMMA: Peacocks have something worth displaying.
NATASHA: [*covering*] Rick. I've heard a lot about you.

> *A bout of tense introductions as* EMMA *is introduced to all.*

Andrew McFarlane as Ron, Emma Jackson as Emma and Kate Raison as Natasha in the 2009 Ensemble production. (Photo: Steve Lunam)

ACT ONE

ROS: We've heard a lot about you, Emma.

Champagne is poured to fill the awkward silence. ROS, *searching for something to say, looks around.*

Is that a new... er?

NATASHA: John Olsen.

ROS: It's wonderful.

NATASHA: I've got a very good person who alerts me when there's a bargain coming up.

ROS: It's beautiful. Isn't it, Toby?

TOBY: Yeah.

ROS: Stunning.

TOBY: I saw this fascinating documentary where they taught chimpanzees to paint and they had the same wonderful free-flowing anarchy.

RON: I doubt if there's a chimp getting over half a million per canvas.

RICK: Over half a million?

RON: That one was seven hundred thousand, but it will be worth twice as much in ten years.

TOBY: Good investment.

NATASHA: We didn't buy it as an investment.

TOBY: The colours do go well with the decor.

RON: How's your work going, Ros?

TOBY: She'd be too embarrassed to tell you but the last three books she commissioned have all become bestsellers. The 'Children Overboard' exposé was huge.

RON: Storm in a teacup.

EMMA: I totally agree.

RICK: A government that lies from the Prime Minister down is hardly a storm in a teacup.

RON: Written by some lefty academic on our tax money no doubt.

RICK: You'd rather spend hundreds of millions teaching some brain-dead young cricketer to improve his line and length at the Institute of Sport?

RON: If it stopped those bloody Indians beating us, I'd spend three times as much.

NATASHA: [*quickly*] So how's that new project of yours shaping up, Toby?

TOBY: It fell over.

RON: What does that mean in money terms?
TOBY: I would say, on the balance of probabilities, disastrous.
ROS: Oh, Natasha. Geraldine Brooks has agreed to come up and talk to us about her last novel. She wants a holiday and she's an old friend.
NATASHA: Ah, that's nice.

Another silence.

RON: You're a musician, Rick?
TOBY: Composer.
RON: Composer?
RICK: Songwriter actually.
RON: What are some of your songs? I might have heard them.
RICK: They haven't been recorded yet.
EMMA: Where does your income come from?
RICK: Collecting glasses in bars.
TOBY: Rick's latest song is amazing. He's on the verge of a big breakthrough.

RICK looks at his dad: 'Don't do that.'

EMMA: I'm glad. Be horrible to have to collect glasses all your life.
RICK: Leaves your mind free. Some of my best songs have come to me while I'm doing it.
ROS: [*to* EMMA] I've heard you're doing very well in the law?
RON: They call her The Terminator.
EMMA: Dad!
RON: Don't mess with her.
RICK: So who do you act for, Emma? Big corporations?
EMMA: Yes.
RON: She's Rupert Murdoch's lawyer of choice.
EMMA: Not for his big deals. Not yet.
RICK: Rupert Murdoch?
EMMA: You've got a problem with him?
RICK: Apart from the fact that his gang of right-wing journalistic thugs attack my father at every possible opportunity, no.
ROS: Rick.
EMMA: Really? On what grounds?
RICK: Because, unlike them, he tells the truth.
EMMA: Except when he gets his facts wrong.
RICK: One fact wrong. His big message is right.

ACT ONE

EMMA: Which is what?
RICK: That the free market lets greed run riot and to hell with the people it shatters and the lives it ruins.
EMMA: Greed is part of the human condition. The free market channels and harnesses that greed to deliver unbelievable prosperity to hundreds of millions.
RICK: And the rest of the world lives on two dollars a day.
RON: Rick, people in superannuation funds have doubled their wealth in the last five years.
TOBY: What about this subprime thing? The mortgage lending mob in the U.S. that's just lost over ten billion?
RON: This isn't 1929, Toby. We know a hell of a lot more about the right economic levers to pull these days. Panic journalism sells papers.
TOBY: Hedge funds managers making almost a billion dollars a year? New York apartments that cost five million a year ago now selling at twenty million? Huge levels of debt. Hasn't the bubble got to collapse some time down the track?
RON: Those hedge funds managers you're bagging have worked out incredibly sophisticated ways to make debt levels totally irrelevant. The market will continue to deliver big time.
RICK: Deliver what? An ecological crisis of humungous proportions, and the gobbling up of our remaining resources...
EMMA: Here we go. Deep green panic.
RICK: Panic? The Arctic icecap has all but gone.
ROS: Please. This is a birthday. A celebration.
EMMA: I'm sorry. I just can't stand kneejerk pessimism.
RICK: Let me tell you something, honey. The world's great hydrocarbon party is drawing to a close.
EMMA: Whatever the problem, technology will solve it.
RICK: Technology can't find energy sources that aren't there.
ROS: Can we perhaps make a move to the restaurant?
RICK: [*to* EMMA] Do you think I *want* a bleak future for our children and their children?
EMMA: From the sound of it, nothing would make you happier.
RICK: Sorry, Dad. These people are fucking dinosaurs. I'll celebrate with you later.
ROS: [*worried*] Where are you going?

RICK: Someplace where there's music and booze.
TOBY: Catch a taxi home, son.
RICK: I will.
TOBY: No really, I worry.
ROS: We both do.

He leaves

EMMA: Sorry, I'm getting out of here too.
RON: Where?

EMMA picks up some car keys.

Hey. Take your mother's Golf.
EMMA: I'm in a BMW mood.

She leaves. There is an awkward silence.

NATASHA: Volatile young man, your Rick.
RON: There's another word for it.
TOBY: Which is what?
RON: Bloody rude.
NATASHA: Ron, don't make things worse.
TOBY: Your daughter *is* a little light on charm.
ROS: Toby.
TOBY: Ros, I'm sorry. This is not going to work.
RON: You're damned right it's not.
TOBY: [*to* ROS] Ring up and cancel that booking.
ROS: Toby.
TOBY: It was a stupid idea in the first place.
RON: Buddy, you are not kidding.
NATASHA: I have to say that Ron is right. Your son was very, very rude.
ROS: And your daughter threw petrol on the flames.
NATASHA: Emma is a highly intelligent woman who says what she thinks and I'm proud of her for it.
ROS: I'm sorry. Toby, let's go.

They head for the door in a stony silence. Just as they're about to get there NATASHA *calls out.*

NATASHA: Ros, about the book club.
ROS: Yes?
NATASHA: We appreciate you have personal connections with high profile writers but—

ROS: But what?
NATASHA: We don't think your friend Geraldine's book is right for us.
ROS: We decided.
NATASHA: Actually you decided.
ROS: I thought everyone was very happy with the choice.
NATASHA: We all tend to think that Carmen Callil was right when she said that Geraldine's prose was a little airport-novelly.
ROS: She's won the Pulitzer Prize, for heaven's sake.
NATASHA: We think it's time to move on to enduring classics. Flaubert's *Madame Bovary*, possibly the most perfect novel ever written. Eva, who spends her summers in Provence, is reading it in the original French.
ROS: I can't believe this.
NATASHA: Some people might see us as provincials up here, but we think our opinions are as good as any.
ROS: In future I'll leave you to discuss them amongst yourselves.

    ROS *and* TOBY *walk towards their car. Suddenly* ROS *erupts.*

We're going back to Sydney!
TOBY: Now hang on.
ROS: You can stay here but there is no way I am living within a thousand kilometres of that woman.
TOBY: I can't go back to Sydney.
ROS: Okay, the press gave you a caning. Totally over the top. Okay, you've been humiliated. What are you going to do? Hide for the rest of your life?
TOBY: You said you were quite happy here.
ROS: I was deluding myself. Sydney is where we belong.
TOBY: I don't belong there. I hate the whole preening, posturing, status-jostling, ego-parading horror of it all.
ROS: You prefer a town full of people whose opinions echo the last Janet Albrechtsen column they read? I want intellectual stimulation again.
TOBY: You can get all the intelligent opinion you need online. *The Guardian*, *New Matilda*, *The London Review of Books*, Crikey, *Prospect*. I get so much intelligent opinion I can't read it all.
ROS: Don't you ever want to discuss it with anybody?
TOBY: I'd have less time to read.

ROS: If you want to be a hermit, fine. I'm going.
TOBY: It wouldn't matter to you if we *were* apart?
ROS: Why would it matter to you? You've got all those journals to read.
TOBY: You know it would matter to me.
ROS: Why?
TOBY: The horror of living in Sydney is quite a lot less than the horror of living without you.
ROS: Occasionally I remember why I married you.
TOBY: Honestly, aren't you overreacting a bit? Join another book club. Noosa's the highest density book club zone in Australia. The women have got to have something to do while their husbands play golf.
ROS: It's not just Natasha. Whenever Rick comes up here I realise how much I miss him. Don't you?
TOBY: [*nodding and sighing*] I'm sure I'll get used to the noise, the dirt, the aggression and the fine particulate matter in the air again.
ROS: Toby.
TOBY: The cancer rates are double what they are up here but we might get lucky.
ROS: I want to be near my son. I want to be amongst stimulating and intelligent friends. I want to feel I'm living again.
TOBY: Okay, okay. We'll go. [*He sighs.*] I really like John Olsen. I just couldn't stand the thought that he had one.

> *In the local bar,* EMMA *is holding a drink. It's a caprioska cocktail. She stares at it malevolently.* RICK *appears, holding a bottle of VB.*

RICK: Are you following me?
EMMA: Yeah, likely. So do you go or I?
RICK: I got here first, honey.
EMMA: That's twice you've called me honey. Don't do it again.
RICK: I'll find another bar.
EMMA: There aren't any. Nightlife finishes at nine. The average age here is sixty-five. You can sit down. I won't bite.
RICK: Promise?

> *He sits down.*

EMMA: This town tries to convince itself it's sophisticated. Are they kidding? They call this a caprioska? Look at the decor of this place.

It's a time warp. The place is still full of bogans. And if I hear them playing Miles Davis's 'Kinda Blue' ever again in a bar, I'll scream.
RICK: You're a really happy person, aren't you?

EMMA *looks at him. She thrusts the caprioska at him.*

EMMA: You taste it. It's shit. They've got to grind the limes. Really grind them. Taste it!
RICK: I wouldn't know the difference. My budget doesn't stretch to caprioskas.
EMMA: Well, get off your arse and get a real job. What kind of degree have you got?
RICK: I haven't.
EMMA: [*staring at him*] No tertiary qualifications? At all?
RICK: I guess it's like discovering a new species for you.
EMMA: You didn't get a good HSC score?
RICK: No, terrible. What about you? Ninety-nine?
EMMA: Point five.
RICK: Sorry.
EMMA: So are you stupid or something?
RICK: No. Dyslexic. If knowledge comes through my ears I'm fine, [*indicating his ears*] but in our education system reading is the only option.
EMMA: So I guess school was pretty terrible for you?
RICK: No, it was great. I spent most of my final year in the music room working the synthesiser. Oh, and Geology. I was very good at Geology. Only subject I sat for. Got top marks. If you want to know anything about rocks, just ask me. I love 'em. Igneous were my favourites. Do you know the derivation of the word 'igneous'.
EMMA: Born of fire.
RICK: How come you only got ninety-nine point five? Did you have an off day?
EMMA: You're quite funny.
RICK: I wish I could return the compliment.
EMMA: Thanks.
RICK: Just stating the bleeding obvious. Whoever ends up with you isn't going to have many laughs.
EMMA: [*angry*] I am funny when I want to be!
RICK: Okay, be funny.

EMMA: I'm not in the mood.

RICK: Why not?

EMMA: Why should I be?

RICK: Apart from one bad caprioska, things seem to be going very well for you. A wealthy family, a stellar career? Although I guess there are tough decisions. Whether to trade up to an apartment with an even better harbour view. Whether to buy the BMW convertible or the Audi?

EMMA: Whatever I've got, I work hard for. You have no *idea* how hard.

RICK: But it's worth it?

EMMA: In general, yeah.

RICK: In general?

EMMA: It has its down moments. The basic premise of the law is to assume that humankind just crawled out of a sewer and the depressing thing is how often that's proved accurate. I've lost count of the number of times I've told my clients to settle because the chances are they're going to lose. But they'd rather fight to the death and pay a fortune in legal fees than admit that the other guy might have a point.

RICK: So why do you do it?

EMMA: The upside is that it can be a huge adrenaline rush. You're working with the big players. The Alpha males. It's like having a herd of Tyrannosaurus Rexes as pets.

RICK: Hang on. Aren't these the same guys who'd rather fight to the death than admit the other guy might have a point?

EMMA: Have you ever heard of the word 'ambivalence'?

RICK: Yes, and you won't believe this. I know what it means.

EMMA: Sometimes the law excites me, sometimes it sickens me. Either way the workload is horrendous.

There's a silence. EMMA *stares straight ahead, and then, surprisingly, she looks a little tearful.* RICK *stares at her.*

Things'll be better when I'm a partner.

RICK: When's that going to happen?

EMMA: Depends how hard I work. It's ordeal by fire, but I'm up for it.

RICK: Good.

EMMA: There's pressure like you wouldn't believe, but I'm up for it. I'm really up for it.

ACT ONE

RICK: Good.
EMMA: But it's not easy.
RICK: I guess not.
EMMA: It's totally full-on. There's too much work and too few people. And your performance is being monitored every day of the week. Billable units. Financial targets. And everything had to be done yesterday. And you spend half your life terrified you forgot something, left something out, forgot to close a loophole.
RICK: What if you do make a mistake?
EMMA: I don't.
RICK: What if you did? What would your pet Tyrannosauruses do then?
EMMA: Rip my head from my shoulders.
RICK: Sounds pretty stressful.
EMMA: You don't get paid what I get paid without there being stress.
RICK: You know what I think?
EMMA: What?
RICK: You're wrecking yourself.
EMMA: I guess life's easy when all you do is collect glasses in pubs. [*She sighs. She knows she's gone too far.*] Sorry.
RICK: I write music.
EMMA: I know. Sorry.
RICK: And that's not easy either. You start with a blank page and have to end up with something that never existed before.
EMMA: At least you do what you want. I just have to do whatever's thrown at me in a workplace that isn't far off toxic. We all smile at each other, but the brutal truth is some of us are going to make partner, some aren't. And the partners go off to golf secure in the knowledge we're all working our butts off. Do you know the rate of depression in the legal profession?
RICK: I'd say about half the rate of out-of-work musicians.
EMMA: Four times higher than the general population. Four times. And women are the worst affected.
RICK: Why's that?
EMMA: Are you joking?

  RICK *shakes his head.*

Apart from the fact that we still have to work twice as hard as a man to be seen as half as good, there is the little question of biology.

RICK *shrugs.*

It's something that you mightn't have noticed, but women have the babies, men don't.

RICK: You want a baby?

EMMA: No, but if I did I've only got a few more years before things start going pear-shaped statistically.

RICK: It's not a worry if you don't want one.

There's a silence.

You do want one?

EMMA: I don't know what the hell I want.

There's a silence.

Two of my friends have had babies.

RICK: So how does that make you feel?

EMMA: I've started to get these images.

RICK: Images.

EMMA: Baby cuddling images.

RICK: They can treat baby hunger. They show baby images and follow them with something truly horrible. In your case maybe a very bad caprioska.

EMMA: [*exploding*] You can joke about it. You can afford to. Men have it so, so easy. You can devote your life to your career, have a ball, get some poor wife to have your child, wave at it every now and then when it's almost asleep, and have the gall to call yourself a parent. I hope in your next life you come back as a woman. A highly intelligent, highly successful woman lumbered with useless primordial instincts that ambush her and turn her life into hell!

RICK: You've got plenty of time.

EMMA: I'm thirty-three! They start testing women for birth abnormalities at thirty-two these days.

There's a silence.

Are your songs any good?

RICK: It's not my opinion that counts.

EMMA: If you haven't sold any they're probably not.

RICK: Which particular charm school did you attend?

EMMA: Don't you get sick of being poor?

RICK: I hate it.

Justin Stewart Cotta as Rick and Emma Jackson as Emma in the 2009 Ensemble production. (Photo: Steve Lunam)

EMMA: [*flaring*] Well, do something about it!
RICK: [*flaring*] What? Study law so I can get to believe that humankind just crawled out of a sewer?

> *They glare intently at each other. Then suddenly kiss. Passionate. Raw lust.* EMMA *breaks away and looks at him.*

EMMA: No. Wrong.
RICK: Why?
EMMA: Too fast. Too sudden. [*Pause.*] Isn't it?
RICK: No.
EMMA: No?
RICK: First rule of life. If there's something you want to do, and you know that it'll make you feel better, but you feel guilty about it…
EMMA: Yes?
RICK: Do it.

> *They look at each other. They're suddenly kissing, even more passionately than before.*

END OF ACT ONE

ACT TWO

EMMA *is sitting on a sofa looking defiant. She's wearing the same clothes she had on the night before.* NATASHA *and* RON *are in dressing-gowns.*

NATASHA: How do you think I felt when I got up and found you weren't in your bed?
EMMA: I'm thirty-three.
RON: Where were you?
EMMA: That's my business.
NATASHA: This is déjà vu. We're not back to those days again, I hope.
EMMA: What days?
RON: You know damn well what days. When we sent you down to Sydney to board at Ascham? Underage drinking, hitchhiking along New South Head Road barefoot at three in the morning—
NATASHA: Almost expelled three times.
RON: Getting involved with coloured kickboxers who could barely talk.
EMMA: If you don't make mistakes how do you learn?
RON: It took you a hell of a lot of mistakes before you learned, young lady.
NATASHA: We thought all those days were over.
RON: Who were you out with and where did you stay?
EMMA: None of your business. I'm getting changed and I'm going out to brunch.
NATASHA: With who?
EMMA: None of your business.
NATASHA: It is our business. Who is he? A Maori nightclub bouncer?
RON: Who are you going to brunch with?
EMMA: Rick.
NATASHA: Oh. Well, thank God for that.

There's a silence, then the information sinks in.

RON: Rick? You weren't—

EMMA *says nothing.*

NATASHA: Darling? He's an out-of-work musician. He collects glasses.

RON: His father's a bloody lunatic leftie.
NATASHA: Darling, you're a top professional. Surely you're not that desperate.
EMMA: I'm having brunch with him. Will you two just stop interrogating me?
NATASHA: Please promise me it's nothing more than that. I couldn't stand the thought of having to be civil to that couple for the rest of my life.
EMMA: I'm having brunch!
NATASHA: Every disaster has a starting point.
EMMA: Can you imagine an out-of-work musician, four years younger than I am, committing to marriage and kids?
NATASHA: Kids?
RON: You want children?
EMMA: I don't know what I want.
RON: Children, great, but not ones carrying genes from that lot.
NATASHA: Sharing a grandchild with those two? That's a horror scenario!
EMMA: I told you. You don't have to worry.

She storms off. They watch her go and look at each other.

RON: They were just both drunk.
NATASHA: Then why are they having brunch?
RON: To call a halt.
NATASHA: I would hope so.
RON: I had to do it all the time in my young days. You dress it up a bit, but you're basically saying, 'Look, I really like you and I don't regret a thing, but I never want to see you again'.
NATASHA: You would've needed all your charm for that one.
RON: Our daughter may be many things but she's not an idiot. When she gets married it will be to a top-line high achiever.
NATASHA: I hope so.

> RICK *enters the living room in smart casual gear.* TOBY *is reading the* Australian *and muttering to himself with rage. He sees his son and speaks up.*

TOBY: Are these guys serious? The polar cap is melting and these idiots are still telling us growth and consumption will go on forever, and printing every climate change sceptic they can still find. Maggie Thatcher didn't retire. She's here editing the *Australian*.
RICK: Why do you read it?

ACT TWO

TOBY: It generates enough rage to propel me through another day. What time did you get in last night?
RICK: Pretty late.
TOBY: Where are you off to now?
RICK: Just into town for a coffee. Bit of brunch.
TOBY: Can we have a talk for just a second?

> TOBY *indicates a seat across from him.* RICK *looks a little worried but sits.*

I'm so glad you came up. I've been worried.
RICK: About what?
TOBY: About you.
RICK: I'm fine.
TOBY: You're not, son. I can tell. It's getting to you. It's getting to me too.
RICK: What's getting to you?
TOBY: You've got real talent, a talent I really believe in, yet here you are at thirty living hand to mouth, collecting glasses at pubs.
RICK: Perhaps I haven't got talent.
TOBY: I heard your latest song. It's great.
RICK: Thanks.
TOBY: But I worry. It's a hugely competitive field you're in. You can have a lot of talent but you also need a lot of luck.
RICK: Yeah, that's what I tell myself, but maybe it's an excuse.
TOBY: Maybe you have to be a little more ruthless. Following your dream sounds like a good thing to do, but it has its pitfalls. Maybe you have to push yourself harder.
RICK: I do everything I can.
TOBY: No. You get a setback and you retreat. You've got to have faith in yourself. You've got to go back again and shake them and say, 'This is fucking good'. You've got to ask yourself why no-talent bands make it and you're still collecting glasses.
RICK: I push myself harder than you think, and it's still not happening.
TOBY: Your music's first-class.
RICK: That's nice, Dad. I appreciate your faith, but—
TOBY: You're good.
RICK: Maybe you've got to be very, very good, very, very original and then very, very lucky on top of that. [*Pause.*] When I was twenty-one I said it'll happen by the time I'm twenty-three; when I was

twenty-three, twenty-five; twenty-five, twenty-seven; but here I am… thirty.
TOBY: Hang in there, Ricki, it'll happen.
RICK: Yeah.

> EMMA *waits for* RICK *at the same coffee lounge their parents met at. He comes. He sits. They look at each other.*

EMMA: Look, I'm sorry. Last night was all a bit crazy.
RICK: Yeah.
EMMA: I mean it was great, don't get me wrong.
RICK: Yeah, it's crazy. I mean it happens in songs—well, not the songs I write, but hey, this is life.
EMMA: I mean it was great. You can't fake—
RICK: No, you can't.
EMMA: But I mean we're old enough not to be impulsive to the point of insanity.
RICK: Yeah.
EMMA: Yeah.
RICK: And I guess the last person your parents want you to get involved with is an unemployed bum.
EMMA: They want me to marry an accountant.
RICK: Sounds sensible.
EMMA: I'm sick of 'sensible'. Do you know what I loved most at school?

> RICK *shakes his head.*

Literature. I wanted to do English at university, but my teachers said I'd just end up a teacher and I was far too smart for that.
RICK: Teacher's *are* seen by some as quite important.
EMMA: I didn't want to be a teacher.
RICK: So now you're a lawyer.
EMMA: What I really wanted to be was a writer, but I knew that that was just a stupid dream.
RICK: Like my stupid dream that I could write songs.
EMMA: Rick, I like you a lot, but it's totally crazy to think we can change our whole life around on the basis of a single night.

> *There's a silence.*

Don't you think?
RICK: Absolutely.

They stare at each other, then suddenly and impulsively embrace.

EMMA, *returns from brunch. Her parents look at her expectantly.*

NATASHA: It's all over I hope?

EMMA: I don't know.

RON: You don't know?

EMMA: Why so surprised?

RON: It's the first time you have 'not known' something since you could talk.

EMMA: I don't know and he doesn't know. Why is it so important to you?

RON: He's an out-of-work musician.

NATASHA: With all the charm of an NRL star on a team-bonding weekend. For God's sake, what's the attraction?

EMMA: We connect.

RON: Connect?

NATASHA: [*to* RON] That's just code for 'good in bed'.

EMMA: It's more than that.

NATASHA: Emma, grow up. If finding someone good in bed was the main reason women got married, the world would be in total chaos.

RON: Hang on here. You told me—

NATASHA: If it was *that* important I'd still be with that personal trainer.

RON: Well, go off and find him!

NATASHA: [*to* EMMA] Darling, we're puzzled. That's all. Puzzled.

EMMA: He listens to me. Every other man I've met just talks about themselves.

RON: That line 'Tell me about yourself' was getting women into bed in the Stone Age.

NATASHA: Emma, what prospects has he got?

RON: He marries Emma and he doesn't need prospects. He wants in on her money and, more importantly, our money.

EMMA: No-one's talking marriage!

RON: He will be, don't you worry. He 'listens' to you, sure. Waiting to hear how much I'm worth.

EMMA: He wouldn't take any of your money. And neither would I.

RON: He won't be getting it. Opportunistic little shit!

EMMA: It couldn't possibly be that he's fallen for me or anything like that?

RON: We love you, love, but you are pretty bloody fearsome.

EMMA: Thanks.
NATASHA: Don't get me wrong. We would absolutely *love* you to get married. Children. All that. Absolutely love it—
RON: But someone who's worthy of you.
EMMA: Well, here's the thing. Women who are 'pretty bloody fearsome' don't exactly get swamped with offers.
NATASHA: Offers? Has Rick made offers?
RON: He's out buying the engagement ring right now.
EMMA: Marriage is not even on the horizon, for either of us. We're not even sure we'll see each other again.
NATASHA: Really?
EMMA: Yes. For God's sake, stop all this panic.

She storms off.

Later, at their house, ROS *and* TOBY *are talking with* RICK.

ROS: Did you have brunch?
RICK: Yeah, with Emma.
ROS: With Emma?
RICK: We got on better than I thought we would.
ROS: What's that mean?
TOBY: What you think it means.
ROS: Emma?
TOBY: She's a Mack Truck whose brakes have failed.
RICK: She's got a vulnerable side.
TOBY: They can all flash a bit of vulnerability when they want something. It's the oldest trick in the book.
ROS: You're going to see her again in Sydney?
RICK: Maybe.
ROS: What's the attraction?
RICK: What is this? An interrogation?
TOBY: Her father's very rich, but…
RICK: Dad, I'm not about to marry her.
TOBY: You're sure?
RICK: Of course I'm sure. I just met her.
TOBY: In your position it could seem like a tempting option.
RICK: In my position? What exactly is that position? A deadbeat? A collector of glasses? A total disappointment. Right?
TOBY: Of course you're not.

ACT TWO

RICK: Now the real truth comes.

ROS: Rick, your father's right. You can't just clutch at the first easy solution that presents itself. You've got to take charge of your life and steer yourself in some definite direction.

RICK: [*passionate*] What definite direction? Tell me. The only thing I know and love is music and you both told me that was great. If you didn't mean it, the time to tell me was back then. Tell me my dreams were fantasies. Tell me to go to TAFE and train to be a dog catcher.

ROS: We don't think your dreams are fantasies.

RICK: Okay, I have thought of marrying her. And maybe it *is* partly because I'm sick of sharing an inner-city slum with two other losers. Living somewhere that isn't knee-deep in cockroaches and being able to write songs has some appeal. Have you any idea how desperate I feel sometimes?

There's a silence.

TOBY: I'm sorry, Ricki. It's your life.

RICK is upset to the point of tears. ROS embraces him. TOBY stands there looking anguished and helpless.

RICK: Look, the chances are remote that this is leading anywhere. And if it does it won't be about money. But if we are right for each other I won't be calling it off because you can't stand her parents.

He goes. ROS and TOBY look at each other.

TOBY: I don't think I was much of a father.

ROS: Toby. I can't think of any other father who's loved his son as much as you.

TOBY: That could've been the problem. Maybe I've done what Willy Loman did to his son Biff in *Death of a Salesman*.

ROS: Which was what?

TOBY: Told him that because everyone likes him, life was going to be easy.

ROS: You never told him that.

TOBY: Yes I did. My speech for his twenty-first birthday. I said something like 'I don't care what Rick achieves or doesn't achieve in material terms for the rest of his life. He's won a place in my heart and his mother's heart for as long as we live, and we're as proud of him as we can possibly be.'

ROS: I still get tears in my eyes when I remember it.
TOBY: It could have been the wrong message.

September 2007.

ROS and TOBY are at a cafe in Glebe in Sydney sipping coffee. RON and NATASHA arrive.

TOBY: Coffee?
NATASHA: No thank you.
ROS: Enjoying your holiday in Sydney?
NATASHA: Not particularly. It's dirty, overcrowded, noisy and polluted. But I guess you feel at home back amongst the chattering inner-city cafe latte elites.
ROS: Yes, it's a pleasure to wake up in the morning and know I'll meet someone who doesn't believe the sun is lodged in John Howard's rear.
RON: John Howard has immense political skills.
TOBY: Indeed. Who else could make the electorate believe that a boatload of sick and dehydrating refugees was a threat to our national existence?
RON: Look, let's not beat around the bush. The only reason we're down here is to talk to you.
ROS: About Rick and Emma?
NATASHA: They're moving in together.
ROS: When people are in love, it occasionally happens.
RON: If your son tried to make something of his life it'd be different, but it's been six months now, and frankly my patience is wearing thin.
TOBY: Your patience?
RON: For six months I've held my breath and hoped against hope Rick would get off his arse, but guess what? He hasn't. He's still earning next to nothing.
TOBY: He's trying.
RON: For God's sake, it's surely clear even to you that he's never going to amount to anything.
TOBY: [*angry*] He's thirty and you can categorically state he's never going to amount to anything?
RON: If your son thinks a marriage certificate is a passport to my money, tell him he'd better think again.

Andrew McFarlane as Ron, Kate Raison as Natasha, Georgie Parker as Ros and William Zappa as Toby in the 2009 Ensemble production. (Photo: Steve Lunam)

ROS: The last thing our son wants is your money. Let's go, Toby. Goodbye, Jocelyn.
NATASHA: Does that make you feel better?
ROS: Actually, yes.

October 2007.

Noosa. NATASHA *and* RON *discuss events.*

NATASHA: [*putting down the phone*] Oh migod. She's pregnant.
RON: Pregnant. As if I didn't have enough problems. The polls are still showing that that economic illiterate, policy wonk Rudd is going to win. Speaks Mandarin? *Konnichiwa.* Wow, big deal.
NATASHA: Ron, it's not helpful to view our daughter's pregnancy as a problem.
RON: What now?
NATASHA: What now, is that she has a baby. That's what pregnancy leads to.
RON: When they've had the baby. What then?
NATASHA: Then we become what are known as grandparents. And when that happens I want us to have an apartment in Sydney so we can go down there.
RON: An apartment in Sydney? Do you know what real estate costs down there now?
NATASHA: I'm not having a situation where Ros and Toby have unlimited access to our grandchild and we see them once a year. I'll get a good agent looking for an apartment overlooking the harbour.
RON: I'm not spending half my time in Sydney. My work's up here.
NATASHA: If she decides not to go back to work she's going to need some help.
RON: She's not going back to work?
NATASHA: She's starting to think she might like to stay at home. But don't say anything yet. She hasn't even told Rick.
RON: Who supports her if she doesn't go back to work?
NATASHA: We do. If she wants to be a mother we should help her.
RON: No!
NATASHA: You'd let your daughter and grandchild suffer to spite Rick?
RON: She hooked up with him. She's got to take the consequences.
NATASHA: Ron, don't be so appalling.
RON: I am *not* paying that bludger to stay idle for the rest of his life.

ACT TWO

NATASHA: I can't understand you. The stock market is at an all-time high and you told me the other day we're worth so much money now that we couldn't spend it in ten lifetimes. What are you going to do with it? Start ten more right-wing think tanks?
RON: It'll go in trust to the grandchildren and he won't be able to get a cent of it.
NATASHA: That's ridiculous.
RON: I'm doing it. I'm seeing my lawyer tomorrow. Our daughter has got to learn that there are consequences. My money isn't about to subsidise the drug habits of an ear-pierced, retro-dressed slackarse like Rick.
NATASHA: Drug habits?
RON: Have you ever read about a muso who doesn't take them?
NATASHA: He does always look a bit glazed around the eyes.
RON: He's on drugs. Bank on it.
NATASHA: Then there's no question. We have to have an apartment in Sydney to make sure Emma's okay.
RON: No.
NATASHA: I'm not looking for anything grand.
RON: No more than a million.
NATASHA: Ron, don't be ridiculous. You can't buy a garage in Blacktown for a million in Sydney. I'll tell the agent not to go over four million.
RON: Four million?
NATASHA: I'm not going to Sydney unless I can see water.
RON: I might not be able to throw money around in the future.
NATASHA: What are you talking about? You said—
RON: Things are good right now but there are some nasty signs.
NATASHA: What?
RON: Merrill Lynch announced a five-point-six billion subprime loss yesterday. It hasn't affected the market yet but it could, and I've got Paradise Sands under construction.
NATASHA: You said they're selling off the plan already.
RON: With the money floating around at the moment you could sell anything. But if times tighten…
NATASHA: You've used award-winning architects.
RON: It's a huge risk, Natasha. Two hundred luxury apartments. If that goes belly up we're wiped. If we have to go to Sydney, let's just stay in a hotel.

NATASHA: Ron, we have to have somewhere for our grandchild to visit.
RON: Bloody grandchild. Not even out of the womb and it's costing me money.
NATASHA: If you're *really* worried, I'll look in the three million range.
RON: Get what you bloody well want. You'll make my life miserable if you don't.

May 2008.

ROS *waits in a cafe, looking at her watch.* RICK *comes in looking preoccupied.*

ROS: I was almost about to go.
RICK: Sorry, Mum, I'm unbelievably busy.
ROS: Doing what?
RICK: Producing a single.
ROS: Your music?
RICK: No. A group of young kids who have potential, but they need whipping into shape.
ROS: Are they paying you?
RICK: Yeah. Not much, but it's a foot in the door. And there is really good money in production if you're right at the top.
ROS: What about your own work?
RICK: I've come to a dead end creatively. I think this is the direction I want to go in.
ROS: Fine.
RICK: Dad'll think I'm selling out.
ROS: It's your life. Whichever way you go, your father is just going to have to adjust.

There's a pause. ROS *is building up to saying something that's been on her mind.*

ROS: Natasha seems to be in Sydney most of the time now.
RICK: Yeah, it's all about the baby. You know. Mothers and daughters.
ROS: It's going to be our grandchild too.
RICK: Of course.
ROS: Apparently Natasha's new apartment is very grand.
RICK: Incredible. Three bedrooms. Huge entertaining area. Views straight down the harbour. Barbeque on the balcony. We had one last night.

ROS: Really. Was Ron there?
RICK: No, he's always up north, thank God. Sitting there with a steak and good red, watching the lights on the harbour. Incredible.
ROS: We do have a barbeque too. Only in a tiny back garden in Glebe, admittedly.
RICK: Mum.
ROS: You and Emma haven't visited us once. The only way we can get to see you both is invite you both to an upmarket restaurant.
RICK: Mum—
ROS: [*fiery*] It is a bit demeaning. Natasha's little Sydney 'pad' is twice as big and hugely more expensive than our one little cottage in Glebe. And it's obvious you and Emma are going to visit every second day.
RICK: Mum. Pregnancy. Mothers and daughters. It's how things work.
ROS: So how long's Emma going to stop working after the baby arrives?
RICK: She's starting to feel that she mightn't go back in a hurry. They still haven't made her a partner and she's staring to feel... over the law.
ROS: Ron will support you, no doubt.
RICK: Ron? He'd rather sing 'The worker's flag is deepest red' than let one dollar of his money ever get to me.
ROS: So how will you support yourself?
RICK: [*shrugging*] I'll face that when I get to it.

Later. ROS *enters her home.* TOBY *looks up.*

ROS: It seems the Princess is giving up work forever and Ron's not going to give them a cent. It's going to put enormous pressure on Rick.
TOBY: Maybe he should feel a little bit of pressure.

ROS *looks at him.*

It *is* about time Rick started to earn some dollars.
ROS: He's trying. He's producing records.
TOBY: Being paid for it?
ROS: Not much yet, but he's learning how to do it.
TOBY: I just wish he'd concentrate on his music. He's got all the talent in the world but he's just not tough enough to push himself.
ROS: He's tougher than you think.
TOBY: When I thought he might have been marrying her for her money I was secretly a little bit pleased.

ROS: Pleased? Why would you be pleased?

TOBY: He *could* concentrate on his music. Stop working in pubs. When I was his age and nothing was coming good for me, I was tempted, I can tell you.

ROS: Who by?

TOBY: Miranda Schwertzer. She was crazy about me. She used to come and pick me up from that grotty flat I shared with my mates. Had an MG sports car. Bright red. Used to let me drive.

ROS: And you almost married her?

TOBY: She was a Schwertzer.

> ROS *looks blank.*

They owned half the commercial real estate in Victoria. Filthy rich. She was no oil painting, but I have to say dynamite in the cot.

ROS: Toby, just what kind of opportunist were you?

TOBY: A desperate one. I tried to get a job, but a pass degree in physics? It was hard to argue that a feeble grasp of quantum mechanics was vital to the future of the meatworkers union.

ROS: You were really going to marry someone you didn't love?

TOBY: Honey, I even got sacked from a job collecting undeveloped films. Went to sleep on the tram. Leapt off. Case flew open and thousands of family memories were crushed under car wheels.

ROS: So that was your solution?

TOBY: It was certainly something I considered.

ROS: Fortunately our son is not as rat cunning as you.

> *She walks off, annoyed.* TOBY *raises his eyebrows.*
>
> *June 2008.*
>
> *Natasha's Sydney apartment.* EMMA, *heavily pregnant, is waiting for* RON *to finish a conversation on his BlackBerry.*

RON: [*on the phone*] You're kidding? Nearly three percent? Resource stocks? [*He listens and shakes head.*] Financials? [*He listens and shakes head.*] Yeah, well gold would be up. When the world is going to shit, gold is always up. [*He hangs up and turns to* EMMA.] Stock market's down again. You're not really going to stop working are you?

EMMA: Yes.

> RON *stares at her.*

RON: Emma, that's crazy. You love your work.
EMMA: I don't really. Not any longer.
RON: Why? You're a gun. You had a setback on the partner thing, but it'll happen. You can't just be a mother.
EMMA: Why not?
RON: You'd be letting yourself down.
EMMA: Letting *you* down, Dad.
RON: What's that mean?
EMMA: My achievements have seemed more important to you than they've ever been to me.
RON: That's rubbish. You loved coming top. You could never stand being trodden on. Just like me.
EMMA: Dad, this may seem amazing to you, but I don't want to be just like you.
NATASHA: Ron, being a mother is the world's most important job.
RON: Emma, you'd go crazy.
EMMA: I was going crazy at work.
RON: It doesn't hurt them to be in day care when they're toddlers.
EMMA: What if I intend to have more than one?
NATASHA: I think it'd be wonderful.
RON: Be it on your own head. That bum is not getting a cent of my money and never will.
NATASHA: That 'bum' is the father of your grandchild.
EMMA: He's also now my husband.

Both NATASHA *and* RON *shriek 'What?'*

NATASHA: But, Emma. When? How?
EMMA: Registry Office.
NATASHA: Emma. Didn't you think of me? One of the things a mother looks forward to most in life is the sight of her daughter in a wedding gown.
EMMA: There was no way we were going to have the full wedding drama.
RON: Don't think this is going to make any difference on the money front.
EMMA: He doesn't want your money. An album he produced has just become a runaway hit.
RON: How much did it earn him?
EMMA: He's making a name for himself.

RON: Yeah, sure.

EMMA: Dad, Rick is the person I love and I believe in him. He wants to see you and have this out.

RON: He wants to see me?

EMMA: Yes, and if you don't sit down and start communicating with him like a civilized human being, then I'm finished communicating with you.

RON: What's he want to see me about?

EMMA: About the future of your daughter and grandchild. He's sick of you underestimating him and treating him as if he's shit!

NATASHA: [*to* RON, *tersely*] Do it, or don't bother coming down here again.

> *A few days later.* RICK *sits at a table in a Sydney coffee lounge. Uncharacteristically, he's dressed neatly and is wearing a jacket and open-necked shirt. There's a briefcase by his side. He has a coffee in front of him. He looks at his watch.*
>
> RON *enters, looks around and, expecting someone more casually dressed, doesn't immediately see* RICK. *Then he spots him and comes over, simmering with anger.* RICK *rises. They greet perfunctorily. When* RON *offers an indifferent handshake, he is surprised by the firm grasp he gets in return.*

RICK: Coffee?

RON: No, had my caffeine quota for today. Look, let's not beat around the bush. I'm going to talk straight.

RICK: Good. So am I.

RON: Emma says she's staying home after the baby arrives and then having more. It's time you got off your arse and started to realise that life isn't a game and started earning yourself some real money.

RICK: I intend to.

> *He reaches down into his case and brings out a folder.*

RON: What's that?

RICK: A business plan.

RON: A business plan?

> RON *almost snatches it off him and starts to read. He grows more and more puzzled.*

It's a business plan.

ACT TWO

RICK: Yeah, I said.

RON: Where did you learn to do a business plan?

RICK: I had the good sense to marry a top commercial lawyer. There's this warehouse in Annandale that's renting really cheaply and it's perfect for a sound studio.

RON: Sound studio? What do you know about sound studios?

RICK: I've been working in one for nearly a year. And there's a real shortage of them in Sydney.

RON: Yeah, I've heard that before. Where's your evidence?

RICK: In there. Appendix C. Rate of growth of hiring costs versus inflation.

He helps him turn to it.

As you can see, the average cost of hire is rising at twice the rate of inflation, a sure sign of chronic shortage of suitable facilities. The income stream projections come from similar start-up studios, but my estimates are deliberately conservative. [*He turns the page and points to the appropriate graphs.*] If you look at the spreadsheet—

RON: Spreadsheet?

RICK: Start-up capital would have to be in the order of two hundred grand—

RON: What's this? You're taking equity without having bloody well invested.

RICK: Ron, it's my concept. I'm not ending up working my butt off growing a business for you and just getting wages. I get thirty percent equity rising to fifty percent in three years if I meet budget projections. Less time if I do better.

RON: Mate, you're an unknown quantity. I'd only give that sort of deal to someone who'd proved himself. I'm not risking two hundred grand when I don't even know if you're any good. Have you seen the stock market lately?

RICK: The last record I produced has become a big hit.

RON: Mightn't have been to do with your production.

RICK: I'll play you the tape they brought to me and I'll play you what happened when I worked it over. You'll think you're listening to a different band. I transformed them and they made the money. Next time I elevate a shit band, they're going to pay for it.

RON looks at him.

Read the rest of the business plan. Even as half owner you'll do very well in the medium term.

RON: Only if all your projections stand up.

RICK: They will.

RON: How come you're suddenly all focussed?

RICK: Because I've finally found out what I'm good at.

RON: How's your father going to feel?

RICK: [*sighing*] Dad's mind's stranded back in the sixties. Fight the system, don't become part of it.

RON: Yeah, chase your dreams, all that shit.

RICK: Yeah. Being 'creative' is a nice sixties thing to do, but I was headed nowhere. Don't ever tell him I told you any of this.

RON: No, no. Of course not.

> RON *looks at the business plan again more positively now after what* RICK *has said, but he's still going to drive a hard bargain. It's in his nature.*

RON: Mate, we're going into tough economic times. Twenty percent equity rising to forty.

RICK: No, mate. I'm not having you in control of the company so you can sell it whenever you choose. It's got to be fifty-fifty.

> RON *looks at him with growing respect.*

> TOBY *waits at a coffee table. He looks at his watch, glances at the newspaper, folds it nervously and looks at his watch again. He's not looking forward to this meeting.* RON *appears. He gets up and they shake hands rather awkwardly.*

TOBY: Coffee?

RON: No. I'm good.

> *There's a silence.*

TOBY: Thanks for coming.

RON: That's fine. What's on your mind?

> TOBY *is obviously on edge.*

TOBY: Your daughter has apparently decided she's never working again.

RON: Don't blame me for that. I told her she was crazy.

TOBY: I understand your objections to giving Rick money, but I'm worried for him. And for Emma. She's apparently going to use all

she's got to put a deposit on a flat. Look, we're not nearly as well-off as you, but if things get tough for them, would you consider going halves with us until he does get on his feet?
RON: You trying to shame me into it?
TOBY: Okay, I know he's not tough. I know he's not competitive, but that's my fault. I brought him up with an unrealistic view of the world.
RON: Yeah, from what I can hear you bagged enterprise, hard work, and self-reliance—every single quality that makes for success.
TOBY: I know. I know. It was the wrong message. But it's obvious that my son loves your daughter very much, and—
RON: Love? That's just something women invented to make guys marry them.
TOBY: I think it's more than that.
RON: You tell me what it is, then.
TOBY: You know you're in love when you think of a person and…
RON: And what?
TOBY: [*thinking*] Smile inwardly.
RON: Smile inwardly?
TOBY: Yes.
RON: Inwardly?
TOBY: Yeah, you sort of say to yourself, 'Hallelujah, thank God I'm with that person'. That sort of feeling.
RON: Is that how you feel about Ros?
TOBY: Yeah, very much.
RON: Lucky you. Believe me, when I think about Natasha, I do not smile inwardly.
TOBY: What do you feel?
RON: About the hits I'm going to take when the credit card account comes in. Do you think Rick smiles 'inwardly' about my daughter?
TOBY: Yes, I think he does.
RON: And there was no thought ever in his head that it might have been a smart move because of our family's wealth?
TOBY: Look, it might have been part of it, but…
RON: 'Course it was and I don't hold it against him. Seizing opportunities is what makes the world tick. In my early years I wasn't having any success at all and I was tempted to marry a rich girl. You come from Melbourne?

TOBY: Yes, originally.
RON: You would have heard of the Schwertzer family?
TOBY: Miranda?
RON: You knew Miranda?
TOBY: Knew her? I almost married her too.
RON: She said her last guy was called… Toby. Good God, that was you?
TOBY: Yeah.
RON: Well, there you go. And let's face it, she was no oil painting.
TOBY: I thought she was *quite* attractive.
RON: I think time has gauze-lensed your memory somewhat, but look, all I'm saying is that we're all human and if Rick had a few dollar bills at the back of his retina, to start off with, then that's not such a bad thing. What I couldn't stand was that he couldn't earn a crust.
TOBY: He was trying to create.
RON: Yeah, well thank God he's given up on that.
TOBY: Given up?
RON: Yeah, I talked to him yesterday. I have to say I had to revise my opinion about that son of yours.
TOBY: Yeah?
RON: Smart as a rattlesnake. I was really impressed.
TOBY: About what?
RON: His business plan.
TOBY: Business plan? Rick?
RON: Really impressive.
TOBY: Business plan?
RON: Mate, your son has got an intuitive entrepreneurial streak a mile wide. Mind like a steel trap.
TOBY: What kind of business plan?
RON: There's a shortage of high quality sound studios in Sydney. He wants to run one.
TOBY: He's a musician. Lives, breathes and dreams music.
RON: He worked out it was a mug's game. One in a thousand succeeds, the rest starve, and one thing's for certain, Rick is not about to starve. He's on his way to becoming the Sir George Martin of Sydney. He knows how you feel about business. He said he respects you a lot, but he's finally worked out that you're trapped back in the sixties dreamtime and that his lefty stance on everything was

ACT TWO

just a desperate desire to please you. I was really impressed with his honesty and frankness. I went over the business proposal with a fine-tooth comb and I couldn't fault it. Mate, to cut to the chase, I've invested two hundred grand in his new studio.

TOBY *is too stunned to say anything.*

Later. ROS *and* TOBY *are talking with* RICK.

TOBY: But, son, he's one of the white shoe brigade.
ROS: He's bulldozing the mangroves to help sell his apartments.
RICK: If it's illegal the regulators should stop him.
TOBY: Regulators? He's in Queensland. Land clearing's a sport up there. Tasmanians have wood chopping, Queenslanders jump in their tractors and clear land.
ROS: His house construction is so flimsy that his developments have to be bulldozed and rebuilt after ten years.
RICK: Mum, that's urban myth. They look fine to me.
TOBY: You'll be beholden to him. If this thing fails he'll sue you and we'll have to try and bail you out.
RICK: If this thing fails. That's what you expect, isn't it?
TOBY: [*unconvincing*] No, but the fact is you haven't had all that much experience in the cut and thrust of the commercial world.
RICK: I know what you think of me, Dad. That I couldn't organise ten seconds silence in a cemetery.
TOBY: I have to say you haven't shown much ability in that direction up to now.
RICK: I wonder why that is?
ROS: Why?
RICK: Because I've been brought up to feel that earning money is the worst of all possible sins.
TOBY: Hey! You always told us all you wanted to do was write songs.
RICK: Well, I tried and guess what? Nobody bought them.
TOBY: Don't lose faith. Your songs are great.
RICK: [*suddenly angry*] What would you know about music, Dad? Your favourite musical was *Hair*. I finally saw it on cable the other night and it's crap. At the end all these hippies who haven't washed for months race on screen singing 'Let the sunshine, Let the sunshine'. Did you really think shit like that was going to change the world?
TOBY: I did.

RICK: I find that hard to believe.
TOBY: So do I. Now.
RICK: Right or wrong, in this society, without money you are absolutely nothing. You don't exist. You're the lowest of the low. You're a ghost who collects glasses in pubs and nobody even notices you're there. Can you understand what that does to you?
TOBY: Yes.
ROS: It's just that Ron is so awful. It hurts me to think he's the key to your future.
RICK: Would you guys have invested two hundred thousand in me?
ROS: He's not doing it for any other reason than he thinks he can make a profit.
RICK: He believes I *can* make a profit. You guys would never have believed.

> *There's a silence. It's true.*

TOBY: I guess it's not as if you're making AK-47s and selling them to the Taliban.
RICK: I could actually be going to produce some music that's going to make life just a little bit more interesting for a lot of people.
ROS: Come to think of it, my great grandfather was a very successful businessman.
RICK: Yeah?
ROS: Made felt hats. But they went out of fashion and he shot himself.
RICK: That's really inspiring, Mum.
ROS: Sorry.
TOBY: When's it all going to start happening?
RICK: Work's starting on the studio in three weeks.
TOBY: I'm sorry, Ricki. It's obvious you're excited about this and that's all that counts. I really hope it goes well.
ROS: We both do.

> *She hugs him.*

RICK: Yeah, I am excited. It's really going to work.

> *September 2008.*
>
> *In their Sydney apartment,* RON *is dialling someone on his BlackBerry.*

RON: Steve mate? Good to hear you. You heard about this Fannie Mae and Freddie Mac stuff. The Republicans are nationalising their banks? What's happening to the world? Stock market's in free fall. How are sales? Of course I'm worried. How are sales? [*He listens.*] Shit. What's happening to the world? Keep in touch. [*He switches off his BlackBerry.*] The stock market's in free fall. Not one enquiry about 'Paradise Sands' today. Not one bloody enquiry.

NATASHA: The stock market's always going up and down.

EMMA enters, carrying a baby.

EMMA: Could you keep the noise down, you two? I'm trying to get Jess to sleep.

NATASHA: [*looking at her adoringly*] She gets more gorgeous every day. Ron, at least you could come and look at her.

He does so reluctantly.

RON: Yes, a huge change from yesterday.

NATASHA: She's got Emma's mouth, can't you see?

RON: I hope she doesn't start to use it as much as Emma does.

EMMA: It's great that you came down, Mum.

RON: I'm here too, in case you hadn't noticed.

EMMA: I've also noticed your huge enthusiasm for your new grandchild.

RON: Let's be frank. They're just a hole at both ends at this stage.

He starts to check his BlackBerry for emails.

NATASHA: Ron, if you're going to turn this place into your office away from home, then go back up north.

RON: Shit! Fifty points down in the last half hour. Has the world gone crazy?

NATASHA: Go home and leave us in peace.

RON: Can I just remind you of your priorities? Wife first, grandmother second.

EMMA: Dad! You're a total dinosaur.

RON: My hard work has kept you and your mother in the lap of luxury. What do you think I am? Just a platinum Amex on legs?

NATASHA: I am staying here in Sydney whenever I want to stay here. Ros gets to see Jess every second day. I'm not going to end up as the grandmother Jess can barely remember.

RON: You two don't get it, or refuse to get it. I'm in trouble. The new development isn't selling anywhere near fast enough.

NATASHA: No wonder. The local radio station has started calling it 'Mosquito Coast'.
RON: That's not the problem anymore. We finally got permission to rip out the mangroves and spray the lake with something that works.
NATASHA: The organic spray didn't work?
RON: It's rubbish. The mozzies race up, eat it, and fly off twice as strong.
EMMA: Get rid of the mangroves?
RON: Don't do the mangrove lover bit. They're muddy, smelly horrible-looking cesspits.
EMMA: They're crucial to the marine food chain.
RON: Since when have you been a bloody green?
EMMA: Since I had a daughter who's going to have to live in the world we leave her.
RON: A few bloody mangroves won't save the world.
EMMA: That's what everyone who's wrecking the world says to themselves.
RON: The reason I'm in trouble has nothing to do with mosquitoes or mangroves. The world is going into total financial collapse. Don't you read the newspapers?

> RON*'s hope that he'll get understanding falls on deaf ears as mother and daughter see the baby smile and are totally delighted.*
>
> ROS *is in a coffee lounge in Glebe, looking at her watch.* RICK *comes in.*

ROS: I was just about to go.
RICK: Sorry, Mum. I'm hellishly busy. Unbelievable. What's on your mind?
ROS: What do you mean, 'What's on my mind'? You haven't even ordered a coffee.
RICK: Mum, I know you. When you call one of these meetings, there's always an agenda.
ROS: All right. As I can see you're frantically busy I won't take up your time discussing life and other irrelevancies. There *is* something bothering me. I'm practically being barred from seeing my granddaughter.
RICK: Mum, you're paranoid.
ROS: I've offered to babysit four times now and Emma has told me she'd prefer her mother to do it.

ACT TWO

RICK: For God's sake, Mum. There'll be plenty of time. Emma and Natasha have bonded very strongly since Jess arrived and there's nothing I can do about that right now.

He looks at his watch.

ROS: Go on. It's obvious you want to be somewhere else.

RICK: Mum, one of the hottest bands in the last ten years is considering letting me produce their next albums. It would be one *huge* step for me.

ROS: Go. For God's sake.

RICK: Okay, I'm on edge.

ROS: They should be glad to have you. You keep telling me you're the best in the business.

RICK: It's not good enough to be the best, you've also got to be able to act being the best. So yes, I'm tense. They've got to come in the door and before they leave believe that I am the best person in the universe to make them even richer than they are now.

ROS: Sorry I've held you up.

RICK: Mum.

ROS: No, you go. I'm sure your father-in-law is feeling very proud of you.

RICK: If you've got issues with Natasha, for God's sake speak to her. I can't solve them for you.

January 2009.

NATASHA *and* ROS *are having coffee. We sense that* NATASHA *is enjoying being in a position of power.*

ROS: I don't want there to be bad feeling between us...

NATASHA: Neither do I.

ROS: But every time I come around to see Jess I feel like I'm an intruder.

NATASHA: That's ridiculous. I'm there a lot I know, but... she's my daughter.

ROS: When I offer to babysit... Emma always wants you to do it.

NATASHA: It's nothing sinister. I just that I know Jess's sleep patterns better.

ROS: [*an edge of anger, almost desperation*] I'm sure I could learn.

NATASHA: [*lying, a touch of triumphantly*] I had no idea you felt this strongly about it.

ROS: She's my grandchild too.

NATASHA: She's going to be six months next week. Why don't you and Toby come to our apartment to celebrate? We just need to see a bit more of each other and I'm sure this thing will sort itself out.

> ROS *isn't at all sure it's the way to sort it out but she has few options.*

> RON *and* NATASHA's *Sydney apartment.* RON, RICK *and* NATASHA *are dressed up ready to go out. They're laughing and joking and having a drink.*

NATASHA: [*to* RICK] Now I know the opera is not really your sort of music, and frankly it's never been mine until recently, but honestly when you give it a chance it overwhelms you.

RICK: Hey, I think I've got a more open mind about this than Ron.

RON: No, I love it. Last time I had the most restful sleep I've had since the stock market crash.

> *They all laugh.* EMMA, *carrying the baby, comes in and sees them all enjoying themselves.*

EMMA: [*tartly*] Have a wonderful evening.

NATASHA: Are you cross, dear?

EMMA: Why would I be cross? I'm looking forward to another exciting evening dragging myself out of bed every two hours to keep your grandchild alive.

RICK: Look, I can take you home if you like?

EMMA: What use would you be? You'd sleep on if a jumbo jet crashed in our backyard.

RICK: I'll fold the cot and take you home.

EMMA: No, you all go out and have fun. Dad's always wanted a son. He's finally got one.

> *She turns and goes back towards the bedroom. They all look at each other.*

> *Some days later.* TOBY, ROS, EMMA *and* RICK *are at* RON *and* NATASHA's *Sydney apartment. They have champagne glasses in hands.* NATASHA *is peering at a photo of Jess adoringly.*

NATASHA: Six months old. Hard to believe time has gone so quickly. She just gets more and more and more gorgeous. I cannot believe it. Can you, Ros?

ROS: [*taking the photo*] Gorgeous. Pity we can't actually see her.

ACT TWO

EMMA: She's been very difficult lately and I've only just got her down.
NATASHA: [*to* TOBY *and* ROS] Go in and sneak a look.
EMMA: Mum.
TOBY: I'd like a peek.
ROS: [*warning*] Toby.
TOBY: I'll go on tiptoe.

> *There's a tense silence as* TOBY *moves offstage. Jessie starts wailing.* TOBY *comes back onstage.*

Why does she always do that when I go near?
RON: She's a very good judge of character.
NATASHA: I have to say, she's the very image of Emma when she was that age. Sometimes I hold her and I think it's time to put my gorgeous little Emma to bed again. I have to say, Ros, not many of Rick's genes seem to have made it through.
ROS: Absolutely none it seems.
NATASHA: Ah well, you might have better luck next time.
ROS: There's a next time planned?
EMMA: Possibly.
NATASHA: There's no financial pressure now that Rick's studio is doing so well.
TOBY: So we hear.
RON: Someone prepared to take a punt on young talent can turn a life right around.
TOBY: Yeah, it was, er, very good of you to take the risk, Ron.
RON: He came to me and I thought, 'Back him. This lad's got more to him than I ever thought.'
TOBY: He's certainly surprised us.
RON: Sometimes parents can't see the talent right there under their noses. Sometimes it takes someone outside the frame.
TOBY: Yeah, I guess.
RON: But look, I'm not here to take all the kudos. Rick has done this himself.
RICK: You've been a big help, Ron.
RON: When I see potential I back it.
RICK: [*getting worn out at having to constantly thank* RON] Yeah. Thanks.
NATASHA: He told me he's a different person now. Every morning he gets up excited about the new day. He can't wait to get to the studio.

RON: It's a great feeling when you can help turn a life around. And I don't mean just the money I invested. Rick, I think you'd admit I've been there for you as a mentor and sounding board whenever you've needed it.

RICK: [*totally without enthusiasm*] You have.

RON: A toast. To a wonderful son-in-law and granddaughter.

> *They drink the toast.*

ROS: How did, er, Paradise Sands finish up, Ron?

RON: Disaster. Fire sale. All but wiped me out. Didn't get as much for our Noosa house as I'd hoped either.

TOBY: Sorry to hear that, Ron.

RON: No you're not. You're bloody delighted, but hey, I'm philosophical. In fact I'm bloody buoyant. With what little cash I did manage to salvage I'm heading off in new directions.

NATASHA: What directions?

RON: You guys will love this. I'm going green.

> TOBY *looks at* ROS.

NATASHA: Green? You always said there's no money in green.

RON: Changing world, my dear. I'm part of a syndicate that's buying up land for carbon-offset trees. The big polluters are going to have to plant eighty thousand hectares a year to be carbon neutral. Big bucks, big bucks. How about that, Tobe? Both on the same side.

> *He smiles broadly at* TOBY. TOBY *winces.*

How's the finance for the new documentary coming along?

RICK: Dad says it's looking really good. The Dutch and the Canadians…

TOBY: The Dutch have pulled out.

RICK: But the Canadians are still in?

TOBY: At the moment.

NATASHA: Maybe if you…

TOBY: What?

NATASHA: Look, I don't want to be insulting, but do your films have to be so gloomy? There are wonderful things about the world. Things to be celebrated. One beautiful grandchild and with any luck more on the way. Isn't that the most wonderful thing? Life is good.

EMMA: If I wasn't still getting woken at twelve, two and four in the morning it might be even better.

ACT TWO 149

RICK: The sleep nurse sorted that out.

EMMA: So why was I up three times last night?

RICK: I paid her five hundred bucks a night.

EMMA: [*tersely*] Well, it hasn't worked.

ROS: I'm sorry to hear that, Emma.

EMMA: [*sarcastically*] Hey, if you guys are enjoying being grandparents that's the most important thing, isn't it?

NATASHA: I'll come over and help you if you want.

EMMA: I'm breastfeeding.

NATASHA: Darling, are you cross with me?

EMMA: When you start announcing new grandchildren without even acknowledging that this one's been horrendous, it does get me a little irritated, but hey, you're all having a wonderful time. Taking Rick to Tetsuya's. Taking Rick to the opera.

ROS: You all went to Tetsuya's?

EMMA: Oh yes. They loved it. Mum tells me that Rick was very funny. Had them laughing all night.

NATASHA: Well, he was. [*To* ROS] I have to say your son is so witty.

ROS: [*to* RICK] The opera?

NATASHA: You loved it, didn't you, Rick?

RICK: [*embarrassed*] Yeah. Ah, it was a lot better than I thought.

NATASHA: We've bought two sets of subscription tickets for the next season so we can all go together. You must love being back here too, Ros?

ROS: Not really. We're selling up and going back up north.

> TOBY *stares at her. First time he's heard it. But he quickly likes the idea.*

NATASHA: You can't be serious.

TOBY: Yeah, we are actually.

ROS: Yes, we're sick of the horrible brown smog you can see hanging over the city every day. I mean we don't have the opera or Tetsuya's up there.

RICK: Mum, stop it. What is this?

ROS: You don't need us around, Rick. I don't know how many times I've offered to help with Jess, but Natasha's always there.

NATASHA: For God's sake, not this again.

ROS: I'd like to see my grandchild occasionally.

EMMA: Ros, the fact that my mother's there doesn't bar you from coming too. The truth is you seem relieved when you hear she's there because you don't have to come.//
ROS: That's so unfair.//
RICK: Emma!//
EMMA: Ask her when's the last time she changed Jess's nappy.//
ROS: I'd do it if you wanted me to.//
EMMA: Sorry, but I don't think so. You might miss the latest art-house movie at the Dendy. And Rick can never do it. He's always working! Or having a night at the opera.//
RICK: Emma, stop it.//
EMMA: [*wound up*] The truth is I couldn't have got through this without Mum. For all I complain she's been absolutely terrific. [*To* ROS] The truth is she's really interested in Jess and you're not.//
ROS: That's not true.//
EMMA: I'm not stupid.//
ROS: If your mother didn't keep telling me how little of our genes made it into Jess, it might be a bit easier.//
NATASHA: [*indicating the baby*] Well, look at her eyes. I can't lie.//
RICK: Emma, in fairness, Natasha *is* at our place an extraordinary amount of time. *I* even feel I don't get enough time with Jess.//
EMMA: What rubbish. At the first wail Jess makes you're out the door, off to your studio. You get more like Dad every day.//
RON: Women are the nurturers, men are the hunter-gatherers. It's nature.//
EMMA: You would have felt really at home in the Stone Age.//
RICK: Emma, it wouldn't hurt to make a little bit more effort to let Mum and Dad into your life.//
EMMA: Why would I bother? They look down on my family from a great height and always have. Okay, my mother doesn't publish books and she doesn't know any Pulitzer Prize winners, but she's here for me when I most need it. If your father and mother are going back up north, frankly I'm relieved.//
RICK: Emma.//
EMMA: They've always been insufferably condescending to Dad and Mum and I can't stand their air of moral superiority. My dad did more for you than they ever did.//
RICK: Emma, calm down. I know you're very stressed—

EMMA: It's true.

RICK: No, it's not. Your father didn't make me feel I was unconditionally loved like my parents did. And they don't expect me to repay them by endlessly singing their praises. Round here I feel like I need a prayer mat. Five times a day down on my knees facing the direction of Ron.

RON: Well, if that's how you feel we'll sell the studio.

RICK: You can't. Read the contract. I've got another two years by which time I'll have at least fifty-five percent of the equity.

ROS: I'm sorry. I think it's time we went.

NATASHA: Don't blame us. I tried to make the peace.

ROS: Yeah sure.

NATASHA: Jealous about who gets to see more of our grandchild? How petty. How ridiculous.

RON: Emma's right. No matter what we do we're wrong as far as you two go. Even when I go green.

TOBY: No. Sounds a great way to rebuild your fortune.

RON: Don't think this little glitch in the world economy proves free market theory was flawed—

TOBY: Yes, we'll soon be back to endless growth and free market paradise. And a totally stuffed planet.

EMMA: [*to* RICK] Just take me home and get me out of this nightmare!

RICK: I'll get the cot.

EMMA: [*to them all*] I'm sorry. This sleep thing has nearly driven me out of my mind.

She breaks down in tears. They all look at each other.

TOBY: [*gently*] I'm sorry about the moral superiority. It shouldn't still be there because I realised the dream of peace, love and understanding was over long ago. But it was such a powerful dream. It felt like a great time to be alive. We were certain that the world was about to change for the better. It was like Obama's election night by a factor of ten. We were wrong, of course. Since the 'Summer of Love' in 1967 there have been a hundred and nineteen wars around the world, but for a brief time there was hope.

He puts a hand on her shoulder. She nods, still in tears. TOBY *and* ROS *leave.*

May 2009.

> TOBY *is at his computer, researching.* ROS *comes in and looks at him.*

ROS: I'm getting to like our new house.
TOBY: Small, I'm sorry, but you lose on stamp duty and taxes every time you shift. But it feels good to be back.
ROS: How was your walk this morning?
TOBY: Fantastic. The sun was sparkling across the water, the waves were that fabulous clear greeny-blue that only happens up here, and dolphins were jumping off Tea Tree Bay.
ROS: [*indicating the computer*] How's it going?
TOBY: The French are in, the Swedes are in, and the Germans are wavering, but it's still looking hopeful.
ROS: Emma's pregnant again.
TOBY: Really? I thought she decided to go back to work?
ROS: She's decided to have one more. She sent me an email. They're coming to see us in six weeks.
TOBY: Really. That's great.
ROS: Yes. They've decided on a name, if it's a girl.
TOBY: [*apprehensive*] What?
ROS: Hope.
TOBY: Hope. That's great. That's really great.
ROS: [*holding out a DVD*] Rick has sent some video shots of young Jessie. Apparently she's the fastest crawler anyone has ever seen.
TOBY: I'll put it on.
ROS: Rick says he's put a bonus track on at the start, especially for you.

> TOBY, *puzzled, puts it on. The final scene of* Hair *begins. We see it on a screen. An empty field suddenly begins to be populated with running figures. Soon the screen is filled with young people in sixties garb singing 'Let the sunshine'. The music swells, the light fades.*

THE END

www.currency.com.au

Visit our website to:

- Buy your books online
- Browse through our full list of titles, from plays to screenplays, books on theatre, film and music, and more
- Choose a play for your school or amateur performance group by cast size and gender
- Obtain information about performance rights
- Find out about theatre productions and other performing arts news across Australia
- For students, read our study guides
- For teachers, access syllabus and other relevant information
- Sign up for our email newsletter

The performing arts publisher

www.ingramcontent.com/pod-product-compliance
Lightning Source LLC
Chambersburg PA
CBHW042129160426
43198CB00022B/2959